D0105895

Thomas Bermingham:
nineteenth-century land agent and 'improver'

Maynooth Studies in Local History

SERIES EDITOR Raymond Gillespie

This volume is one of six short books published in the Maynooth Studies in Local History series in 2018. Like their predecessors they range widely, both chronologically and geographically, over the local experience in the Irish past. Chronologically they span the worlds of medieval Tristernagh in Westmeath, a study of an early 19th-century land improver, the Famine of the 1840s in Kinsale, politics and emigration in the late 19th century and sectarian rituals in the late 19th and 20th centuries. Geographically they range across the length of the country from Derry to Kinsale and westwards from Westmeath to Galway. Socially they move from those living on the margins of society in Kinsale and Galway in the middle of the 19th century to the politics and economics of the middle class revealed in the world of Thomas Bermingham and the splits in Westmeath in the 1890s. In doing so they reveal diverse and complicated societies that created the local past, and present the range of possibilities open to anyone interested in studying that past. Those possibilities involve the dissection of the local experience in the complex and contested social worlds of which it is part as people strove to preserve and enhance their positions within their local societies. Such studies of local worlds over such long periods are vital for the future since they not only stretch the historical imagination but provide a longer perspective on the shaping of society in Ireland, helping us to understand the complex evolution of the Irish experience. These works do not simply chronicle events relating to an area within administrative or geographically determined boundaries, but open the possibility of understanding how and why particular regions had their own personality in the past. Such an exercise is clearly one of the most exciting challenges for the future and demonstrates the vitality of the study of local history in Ireland.

Like their predecessors, these six short books are reconstructions of the socially diverse worlds of the poor as well as the rich, women as well as men, the geographical marginal as well as those located near the centre of power. They reconstruct the way in which those who inhabited those worlds lived their daily lives, often little affected by the large themes that dominate the writing of national history. They also provide models that others can follow up and adapt in their own studies of the Irish past. In such ways will we understand better the regional diversity of Ireland and the social and cultural basis for that diversity. They, with their predecessors, convey the vibrancy and excitement of the world of Irish local history today.

Maynooth Studies in Local History: Number 138

Thomas Bermingham: nineteenth-century land agent and 'improver'

Cathal Smith

FOUR COURTS PRESS

WITHDRAWN FROM
EMORY UNIVERSITY LIBRARY

Set in 10pt on 12pt Bembo by
Carrigboy Typesetting Services for
FOUR COURTS PRESS LTD
7 Malpas Street, Dublin 8, Ireland
www.fourcourtspress.ie
and in North America for
FOUR COURTS PRESS
c/o IPG, 814 N Franklin St, Chicago, IL 60622

© Cathal Smith and Four Courts Press 2018

ISBN 978–1–84682–720–4

All rights reserved. Without limiting the rights under
copyright reserved alone, no part of this publication may
be reproduced, stored in or introduced into a retrieval system,
or transmitted, in any form or by any means (electronic,
mechanical, photocopying, recording or otherwise), without
the prior written permission of both the copyright
owner and the above publisher of this book.

Printed in Ireland
by SprintPrint, Dublin.

WITHDRAWN FROM
EMORY UNIVERSITY LIBRARY

Contents

Acknowledgments

The bulk of the research for this study was undertaken during the course of my doctoral studies at the National University of Ireland, Galway. I wish to thank my PhD supervisor, Professor Enrico Dal Lago, for all of his encouragement with this project. NUI Galway's history department has been an ideal context in which to research and work for the past several years, due primarily to its staff and students. Among those who have been instrumental in providing crucial insights into the topics dealt with in this volume have been Dr John Cunningham, Dr Niall Ó Ciosáin, Dr Kevin McKenna, Dr Conor McNamara, Dr Kevin O'Sullivan, Dr Sarah-Anne Buckley and Dr Brian Casey. My ideas here have also been shaped by participation in the 'historians of intervention' research cluster associated with the Centre for the Investigation of Transnational Encounters (CITE), which is based at the Moore Institute, NUI Galway. I also wish to acknowledge the Irish Research Council for generously funding my doctorate, and the staff of the National Library of Ireland for facilitating access to many of the sources on which this study is based. Finally, I must express my sincere gratitude to my family and friends for their constant support. Gerard, Caitríona, Brían, Declan and Richard have all been helpful in myriad ways; Brian and Anne deserve thanks beyond measure.

Introduction

Between the end of the Napoleonic wars in 1815 and the beginning of the Great Famine in 1845, Ireland was a country on the brink of crisis. The Famine was by no means inevitable, but even before the arrival of the potato blight there was widespread recognition throughout the United Kingdom that Ireland's socioeconomic system was beset by deep structural problems. Together with the well-known religious and political divisions in Irish society, the country's depressed economy – agriculturally dominated and geared primarily toward export to Britain – its rapidly increasing population, and the seemingly endemic poverty of a large proportion of its inhabitants were all troubling issues for politicians and policy makers at Westminster. Ireland was thus a persistent topic of debate and discussion in Britain during the first half of the 19th century.[1]

Within Ireland, too, there emerged a cohort of self-proclaimed 'improvers' who proposed various answers to the 'Irish question'. While the proposals of these disparate reformers varied, Irish social and economic modernization was their unifying aim.[2] Prominent among these 'improvers' was Thomas Bermingham, a land agent best known for his management of the Clonbrock estates in counties Galway and Roscommon between 1826 and 1843. As well as attending to this occupation, Bermingham also spent much of his time campaigning for the reform and improvement of Irish agriculture and wider society. During the 1830s and 1840s he participated in several committees and societies, while also publishing many pamphlets in which he gave his opinion on various topics, including estate management, landlord–tenant relations, and the need for investment in Irish infrastructural development. Perhaps the scheme for which Bermingham gained most notoriety in his day was his campaign for the construction of an Irish rail network; his tireless action in this sphere was such that it earned him the sobriquet 'railway' on at least one occasion.[3]

Yet, despite Bermingham's prominent profile in early Victorian Ireland, little of substance has hitherto been written about him, with the notable exceptions of Kevin McKenna's work on the Clonbrock estates and Patrick Melvin's discussion of Bermingham's activities in his *Estates and landed society in Galway*.[4] Thomas Bermingham is thus a ripe candidate for study, since he was simultaneously a professional land agent and a reform-minded lobbyist, public and private roles that could be both complimentary and contradictory. His career offers an opportunity to gain new insights into the history of Irish land agents – a subject that has recently captured the attention of several scholars – as well as indigenous efforts to modernize Ireland in the years before, during, and after the Great Famine (1845–52).⁵

Thomas Bermingham's occupation as a land agent is perhaps unsurprising, considering that he was the son of Walter Bermingham, onetime agent to Lord Clanricarde in county Galway.⁶ Thus, the young Thomas Bermingham would have been exposed to the expectations and demands of a land agent both as a manager of landed estates as economic enterprises and a mediator between landlords and tenants. Bermingham could also claim a famous family member; he was a nephew of Henry Grattan, who led the Irish patriot movement of the 1770s and 1780s and successfully agitated for legislative independence for the Irish parliament in 1782.⁷ The picture of Thomas Bermingham that emerges from the archives – including his pamphlets, the Clonbrock estate papers, the many parliamentary commissions to which he gave evidence, contemporary newspapers and the publications of the committees with which he was involved – is one of a well-informed and ambitious, if somewhat egotistical, individual. He brought a professional but pragmatic outlook to the Clonbrock estates in Galway and Roscommon, where he fulfilled the role of not only a collector of rent, but also a manager, a dispenser of charity, and an architect of 'improvement'. From the early 1830s on, he also projected his improving ethos onto wider society by participating in agricultural societies and infrastructural improvement schemes that aimed to modernize Ireland's economy.

Thomas Bermingham's historical status as an 'improver' implies that the society in which he lived needed improvement. By whatever barometer one chooses to measure conditions in pre-Famine Ireland, it appears that the economic situation in large parts of the country required amelioration. In his youth and early adulthood, Bermingham would have witnessed the sea-change in Irish economic fortunes that occurred after 1815. In the late 18th and early 19th centuries, during the Revolutionary era and Napoleonic wars, Irish agricultural produce, particularly grain, enjoyed generally high prices on British markets. As a result, this era witnessed a shift – though not a wholesale one – from livestock to tillage farming as the Irish economy responded to the dictates of domestic, British and world markets. While this period was relatively profitable for landlords, middlemen and tenant farmers, agriculture was generally not efficient. Glaring flaws existed that were exposed following the cessation of war in Europe in 1815, when Irish agricultural commodities became increasingly subjected to foreign competition. This problem was further exacerbated as England – the chief market for Irish agricultural produce – moved toward a free trade position as it industrialized in the first half of the 19th century. Ireland's population also rose rapidly after 1750 and continued to increase despite the depression in agricultural prices that characterized the decades succeeding Waterloo. The resulting competition for land encouraged the subdivision of holdings, the sub-letting of land to cottiers, and the conacre system – whereby small plots of land were rented by labourers for a year at a time in order to grow subsistence crops, usually potatoes. Consequently, access to land and agrarian issues were often at the root of the violent acts perpetrated by secret societies such as the Ribbonmen, the Whiteboys and the Rockites in different parts of pre-Famine Ireland.[8]

In the decades after 1815, the disturbed and impoverished condition of rural Irish society became a pressing concern at Westminster. Parliamentary commissions, such as the Poor Inquiry of the mid-1830s and the Devon commission of the mid-1840s, attest to the official recognition of the problems of widespread Irish poverty and land tenure.[9] It was in this context that various British political economists, including David Ricardo and Thomas Malthus, began to focus on the 'Irish question'. Most of these commentators advanced the view that Ireland should be 'anglicized', with farms consolidated into larger units and small tenants and cottiers transformed into wage labourers. Discussing Ireland in an 1817 letter to Ricardo, for example, Malthus wrote that 'a great part of this population should be swept from the soil into large manufacturing and commercial towns'.[10] However, Malthus failed to appreciate that, apart from north-east Ulster, by the 1820s Ireland had no industrial sector capable of absorbing the 'surplus' population that would have been created by the widespread consolidation of small holdings. In fact, much of Ireland was actually de-industrialized in this era as linen manufacturing – formerly diffused throughout the country – became centralized in Belfast and its hinterland.[11] Recognizing this, later British commentators, such as Robert Torrens, placed their faith in emigration as a panacea for Irish ills. While emigration, both voluntary and assisted, did indeed increase in the decades before 1845, it was usually the more prosperous farmers who left, and the net population continued to rise. In these circumstances, more and more people lived at subsistence level and became dependent on the potato for their survival.[12]

Unsurprisingly, in the midst of this sustained economic downturn, there were voices calling for reform and modernization within Ireland. 'Improvers' from various backgrounds emerged and proposed schemes for the amelioration of the Irish economy. Individuals including William Conner, William Blacker, Robert Kane and William Sharman Crawford followed in the footsteps of Samuel Madden, an influential member of the Royal Dublin Society, who, a century earlier, had preached of Ireland's economic potential if it were to be 'improved'.[13] Thomas Bermingham can be numbered among this milieu. More familiar with conditions as they existed in Ireland than British economists and politicians, and understanding the unlikeliness of wholesale clearances of the small farmers and cottiers who predominated on landed estates in many parts of the country (at least before the Famine offered an opportunity to do so), these Irish reformers set out to ameliorate things as they stood in practice, rather than indulging in the theoretical musings of Ricardo, Malthus, et al.[14] Recognizing that small holders and cottiers were an entrenched feature of Irish agriculture, the improvers of the pre-Famine era, while influenced by British agriculture in many ways, also pointed to continental nations, such as Belgium, as proof that small holdings were not necessarily impoverishing if they were farmed intensively, if modern agricultural implements could be introduced, and if the more remote regions of the country were connected to local, national, and international markets through the introduction of a coordinated transportation network.[15]

It must be emphasized at the outset of this study that 19th-century Ireland's 'improvement' movement was by no means benign or benevolent in motivation, incidence, or effect. Although its ideologues and practitioners held that 'improvement' would be beneficial for all classes, it was primarily in the interest of the landed elites, who were anxious to implement reforms that would better their position in rapidly globalizing world markets and thereby safeguard their wealth. Bermingham appears to have been among those Irish 'improvers' who truly believed in both the necessity for agricultural and infrastructural modernization and their prospective social benefits, but the 'reforms' that stemmed from this belief led to misery and dislocation for countless farmers, labourers and their families. This was especially the case during the Famine, when the rhetoric of 'improvement' was used to justify the evictions and clearances enacted on many estates with a view to using the crisis to accelerate agricultural modernization.[16] Together with the paternalistic ideology that was ascendant among the Irish landed class during the 19th century, 'improvement' was a conservative phenomenon designed to rationalize and perpetuate the fundamentally exploitative status quo.

Land agents were logical candidates to formulate and implement the various schemes that grew out of 19th-century Ireland's culture of 'improvement,' since they were at the coal face of the country's agricultural system. It was William Blacker, an Ulster land agent and a contemporary of Bermingham's, who advised Irish farmers to adopt 'green-cropping' – whereby tillage crop rotations were to include turnips, clovers, vetches and artificial grasses, which could be used to house-feed livestock and generate manure – by proving its utility on the estates of the earl of Gosford and Colonel Close in Armagh.[17] Blacker's innovations built upon international developments in agricultural science and practice, particularly in Britain, but tailored them to local Irish conditions. The popularization of his green-cropping system during the 1830s and 1840s contributed to a slow and uneven revolution in Irish farming techniques.[18] This, in turn, was part of a larger project envisioned by 'progressive' members of the landed class to consciously modernize and 'improve' their rural economy and society. Thomas Bermingham is another land agent who left his mark, not only on the estates that he managed, but also on the wider movement for elite-led 'improvement' that rose to prominence in Ireland during the decades that followed Waterloo.

1. Thomas Bermingham, professional land agent

While the traditional picture of Irish landlords saw them depicted as rapacious pariahs and absentees, recent scholarship has provided a more nuanced picture of their behaviour – one that emphasizes diversity and change over time.[1] It is true that Irish landlords were often detached from the running of their estates during the 17th and 18th centuries; however, the economic downturn of the post-Napoleonic era saw many, though not all, landowners take a more active interest in the running of their properties.[2] By doing so, they contributed to the emergence of a phenomenon that I have elsewhere called the 'second landlordism', which encapsulates the movement for agricultural modernization that became increasingly prominent in Ireland during the decades after 1815 in response to the economic depression that followed the Napoleonic wars and the transformation of global capitalism associated with the industrial revolution.[3] Land agents played an important role in this second landlordism. While Irish landowners had long employed agents to collect rent and manage their affairs, prior to the 19th century agents were frequently either large tenant-farmers or members of the gentry and often possessed little business acumen. Just as landlords have been cast in popular consciousness as oppressors of a helpless peasantry, so too have their agents traditionally been seen as exploitative predators – a stereotype perhaps best exemplified by the villainous character Garraghty in Maria Edgeworth's *The absentee*, and by their portrayal in William Carleton's 1845 novel *Valentine McClutchy*.[4]

Just as historians have provided us with a more nuanced understanding of Irish landlords, so too should we recognize complexity among Irish land agents, especially after 1815, when a professional, business-minded cohort began to emerge. According to a range of historians, including K. Theodore Hoppen, Ciarán Reilly, W.A. Maguire and Desmond Norton, the post-Napoleonic period witnessed the rise of a new generation of professional agents in Ireland – men with entrepreneurial and organizational skills whose primary responsibility was the ordering of their employers' affairs. As landlords increasingly took direct control of their properties from the 'middlemen' who had been a notable feature of Irish estate management during the 18th century, they desired the service of agents whose responsibility was not simply to collect rents and enforce evictions, but also to run their properties as commercial agrarian enterprises. Hence, a new generation of professional land agents replaced the middleman system, which was gradually phased out in the first half of the 1800s.[5]

Recognizing the long-term instability of the Irish landed estate system as it stood after 1815, and responding to a mixture of persistent economic depression, intermittent social unrest, and the growing criticism of their perceived ineptitude, increasing numbers of Irish landlords began to employ professional agents with a view toward maximizing the economic potential of their properties. The emergence of centralized land agency firms, including Stuart and Kincaid, Guinness, Mahon, Hardy & Co., and Samuel Hussey – which established sophisticated administrative bureaucracies in order to manage estates for multiple clients throughout the country – are a striking example of this fresh emphasis on professionalization within Irish estate management in the post-Napoleonic era. Some among this new generation of land agents deservedly earned negative reputations for their excessive focus on profit at the expense of small farmers and cottiers, whom they were often accused of heartlessly evicting in a blind drive for modernization.[6] However, land agents could also be found throughout 19th-century Ireland who worked for a version of 'improvement' that aimed to rationalize estate management and modernize agricultural production while simultaneously retaining the paternalistic bonds of loyalty that they typically believed existed between landlords and their tenants. Thomas Bermingham was one such individual. His career allows us to investigate the outlook and behaviour of the professional land agents that rose to prominence in Ireland during the first half of the 19th century.

According to John Cannon Evans, a contemporary of Bermingham's and a fellow land agent in the east Galway region, it was the duty of every agent

> to consider himself as the representative of the landlord, and in every instance to embrace every opportunity of knowing what measures he can and ought to adopt to benefit the property and the tenantry thus committed to his care – to look after the improvement of the soil, and the receipt of the rents, and besides, to look to the moral as well as the physical improvement of the different families – to encourage industry and virtue, to discourage idleness, to punish vice, and to take pleasure in seeing the landlord's property improve, and the tenantry happy and contented.[7]

Of course, fulfilling these duties was easier said than done, since the dual imperative of an agent to act in the best interest of the landlord and simultaneously 'care' for the tenantry often came into conflict. By the early 19th century, many Irish landed estates, especially in the west and south-west, had become sub-divided and held by tenants, under-tenants, and cottiers who lived at a subsistence level, and whose farming practices damaged the soil by planting repeated grain crops in an attempt to extract the maximum short-term monetary return from their holdings. In dealing with this precarious situation – one complicated by the deep sectarian divisions in Irish society at the time – land agents had to walk a tightrope between the interests of their employer and the interests of the tenants. The practical results of this dilemma can be seen through the prism of Thomas Bermingham's career as agent for the Clonbrock estates in counties Galway and Roscommon between 1826 and 1843.

The Dillons of Clonbrock traced their lineage in Ireland to 1185 when one of their ancestors – Sir Henry de Leon – arrived in the wake of the Anglo-Norman invasion, subsequently settling in Westmeath and becoming part of 'the Pale's' landed gentry. In the late 16th century a branch of this family established themselves in east Galway. Having survived the wars and confiscations of the 1600s, they converted from Catholicism to Protestantism in the 1720s to avoid the negative effects of the penal laws. In 1790, Robert Dillon (1754–95) was granted the hereditary title Baron Clonbrock by the Irish parliament.[8] In 1826, following the death of Luke Dillon, 2nd Baron Clonbrock, his eldest son Robert (1807–93) became the 3rd Lord Clonbrock. His property was largely situated in the vicinity of his home in Ahascragh, Co. Galway, but he also inherited smaller estates in Roscommon, Limerick, Westmeath and Tipperary. In total, Clonbrock was estimated to have owned over 28,000 acres of land and was one of 19th-century Ireland's wealthiest men.[9] Around the time of Luke Dillon's death, Thomas Bermingham began his employment for the young Baron Clonbrock. By then, Bermingham was already an experienced land agent. From at least 1815, when the first documentary evidence relating to his career can be found, he managed estates in counties Laois, Longford and Monaghan on behalf of his uncle, Henry Grattan.[10] After Grattan's death in 1820, Bermingham was employed by Ross Mahon, an absentee landowner with property in east Galway and south Roscommon.[11] From 1826 on, as agent for the Clonbrock estates, Bermingham was established at the head of a retinue of employees and administrators, including the steward Bryan Finaghty (later succeeded by Henry Wheatley), Thomas Blackstock, agent for the Quansbury and Bermingham estates in south Galway, and James Kelly, agent for Clonbrock's Limerick properties.

By the time of Robert Dillon's coming-of-age celebration in April 1828, Bermingham was named as the primary agent for the Clonbrock estates in the press; according to the *Freeman's Journal* he 'seemed on this, as on all other occasions, to evince the very strongest and most zealous anxiety for the happiness of the tenantry and the ardent desire to render everything agreeable'.[12] In November 1830, Clonbrock delegated the management of his affairs into Bermingham's exclusive control, writing that 'no orders shall be given by any person in my employment but by Mr Thomas Bermingham.'[13] Thus, Bermingham took command of a vast and complicated estate enterprise on his employer's behalf, with responsibility for collecting rents, letting land and renewing leases, organizing evictions and notices to quit, implementing improvement schemes and long-term investments, ensuring the solvency and profitability of the estate, negotiating the purchase and sale of property, dispensing charity to the poor, sick and infirm, and overseeing the fortunes of Clonbrock's personal farming and forestry operations.

Bermingham's superintendence of Clonbrock's affairs was particularly all-encompassing the first seven years of his agency, when he was not only responsible for estate management, but also ran 'the place,' including the big house, gardens, demesne farm and forests. From 1827 to 1833, with Bryan Finaghty apparently ineffectual in the role of steward, Bermingham entered into the minutiae of the demesne's administration, right down to providing specific instructions for Clonbrock's bailiff, shepherds, carpenters, woodrangers and other employees. This can be seen from the detailed directions that he recorded in the estate, farm, and household account books, which show Bermingham's role in the day-to-day management of the 'big house' and demesne.[14] Evidently, in order to manage the place effectively, Bermingham left a surrogate at Clonbrock House as his proxy, writing in May 1827: 'whilst Bryan Finaghty is unwell I leave John Callanan at Clonbrock that he may see that my various orders about the place are executed exactly'. Bermingham soon used Finaghty's ill health as a pretext to strip him of all authority; in reality, however, the agent appears to have been punishing the steward for what saw as disobedience. In June 1827, Bermingham recorded that Finaghty had countermanded a direct order by sanctioning shearing on a different day from that dictated by himself, and immediately thereafter: 'as Finaghty's health is so delicate, I wish him not to resume the care of this place, nor to take any part therein for some time to come … I consider Callanan responsible to me & me only for the due performance of every direction left by me'.[15] In 1833, Henry Wheatley replaced Bryan Finaghty as Clonbrock's steward, and assumed responsibility for managing the big house and demesne farm.[16] Thereafter, Bermingham took a back seat with regard to 'the place', and directed his energies largely toward the management and improvement of his employer's various estates.

Between 1825/6 and 1830 Bermingham was also responsible for the management of the Wandesforde colliery near Castlecomer in Kilkenny.[17] He later described how he initially found this mine 'in a very dilapidated state. It seemed very ill-managed, the system pursued was as bad as possible; the state of destitution of the working collier was almost beyond endurance.' In response, he employed experts from Newcastle-Upon-Tyne to introduce a new system of mining in the area. This was initially resisted, to the point where Bermingham's life was threatened; on one occasion, he later recollected, 'the numbers collected round me were some thousands, and they attempted or showed every desire to throw me into a pit, and had a coffin prepared for me'. However, he claimed to have been able to convince the local miners that his reforms were in their interests. In 1830, Bermingham proposed to lease the mine from its owner for £1,000 per year, but his offer was refused.[18] He subsequently concentrated primarily on the Clonbrock estates, which he administered from his home in Caramana, Kilconnell, Co. Galway. To these estates he brought the same business-like but pragmatic attitude that had, according to his own account, brought prosperity to the colliery with which he had been associated.

The 3rd Baron Clonbrock, like his father before him, proved to be an improving landlord with a paternalistic mindset.[19] Thomas Bermingham was therefore an ideal agent, since he demonstrated a progressive ethos that went hand-in-hand with Clonbrock's agenda to better the condition of his estates and his tenants. Like all agents, he was expected to cater to the needs of both his employer and the tenantry. In his dealings with Clonbrock's tenants, Bermingham endeavoured to present himself as firm but fair, once remarking that 'I believe they look on me as a friend as much as anything else'.[20] Upon first entering into Clonbrock's employment he reportedly advised the use of leases to bind tenants to improve their land, but subsequently backed down on this issue. According to the Poor Inquiry:

> Mr Bermingham, acting as Lord Clonbrock's agent, at one time proposed to insert clauses enforcing an improved course of tillage in the leases which he made. He, however, relinquished the idea by the advice of His Lordship's new advisers, who objected to the practice on the principle that it was fundamentally wrong to bind tenants to anything of which they were not convinced of the utility either to themselves or their landlord.[21]

Exhibiting the social conscience that would repeatedly emerge in his pamphlets, Bermingham consistently endeavoured – though not always successfully – to steer a course between enlarging holdings and simultaneously treating the farming classes that inhabited Clonbrock's several estates in Galway and Roscommon with respect and humanity. His charitable outlook also extended to landless labourers; as he said on one occasion: 'if a pauper runs up a cabin during the night upon a corner of your land, or in any ditch, how can you take the shelter from over his head?'[22] Generally, however, Bermingham believed that employment and not charity should be extended to such poor people, both by landed proprietors and by the government.[23]

While Bermingham can be appropriately characterized as a socially-conscious land agent who strove to improve the condition of Clonbrock's tenants and labourers, he could also be strict when he felt it necessary. In 1831, for example, he wrote: 'I will not pay any of the labourers until John Mason sees to the state of their houses and yards being in order and where necessary … and if they object to pay it serve them with notices to quit'.[24] The same year, in response to the disturbances engendered in Galway by the agrarian secret society known as the Terry Alts, Bermingham called a meeting of the local tenantry and warned them to combat the agitators; as he told a parliamentary inquiry in 1832:

> I certainly did endeavour to keep the people from transgressing the law, by telling them this: 'if in such a place as Cappatagal [one of Clonbrock's estates] you do not arm yourselves with pitchforks and sticks, and beat back those men who are attacking my Lord French's stock, it will be worse

for you,' and I got them to join me in it heart and hand. I said, 'if you allow such people come in there, I will stop the buildings on the estate, and the drains and the improvements, and leave you to the military.'[25]

Thus, in his dual role as almoner and punisher, Bermingham fulfilled a crucial role in the functioning of the reciprocal duties and rights that underpinned the paternalistic ethos evident on the Clonbrock estates during the 19th century.[26]

One of Bermingham's most important early tasks as Clonbrock's agent was to oversee the purchase of new lands with income generated from the sale of older property, as his employer attempted to shed himself of his distant estates and use the proceeds to purchase land closer to his home in east Galway. The 3rd Baron Clonbrock's mother, Anastasia, was the daughter of Lord Wallscourt of Ardfry, Co. Galway, and a granddaughter of her son's agent's namesake, Thomas Bermingham, Lord Athenry and earl of Louth, who had died without a male heir in 1799.[27] Through this family connection Clonbrock inherited a portion of the Bermingham estate near Athenry in 1827, which he soon decided to sell.[28] It fell to Thomas Blackstock to organize the division and sale of this property, while Clonbrock also sold his Limerick, Westmeath, and Tipperary estates in the late 1820s and early 1830s. At the same time, Clonbrock demonstrated an interest in the purchase of Galway land at Dalystown, Castlegar, Doone and Ballydonelon, whose purchases Bermingham negotiated and whose administration he assumed responsibility for once they were bought.[29] As Clonbrock sold his smaller properties he also shed his smaller agents. By the mid-1830s, therefore, Bermingham was in charge of a more centralized group of estates than the Galway branch of the Dillon family had hitherto owned.[30]

As well as buying and selling land after his inheritance, Robert Dillon, 3rd Baron Clonbrock, also desired to improve the standard of farming on his estates, new and old. It fell to Bermingham to oversee the various resulting improvement schemes. Luke Dillon, 2nd Baron Clonbrock, had engaged in large-scale drainage on portions of his land in the 1820s, and his son followed that example with Bermingham's enthusiastic support and oversight.[31] Clonbrock regularly granted small sums to those of his tenants who invested in draining their own holdings, but the most extensive drainage schemes on his estates involved the reclamation of bogland at Doone, Crith and Castlesampson.[32] In his 1836 report on the state of agriculture in the Kilconnell region of east Galway, Charles Clarke recognized these endeavours, writing that 'it would be a great omission not to notice the great improvements at Crith Bog, now in progress by Lord Clonbrock, under the care of his benevolent and enterprising agent, Mr Bermingham'.[33] An 1835 letter from a renowned English drainage expert likewise placed the agent at the heart of these efforts, stating that it was because of Bermingham's 'recommendation [that] my Lord Clonbrock commenced his improvements at Crith Bog'.[34] As such, Clonbrock and Bermingham were leading participants in the wider drive for drainage and wasteland reclamation that became common among improving Irish landlords in the second quarter of the 19th century.[35] Furthermore, they both explicitly called for others to emulate their behaviour in this respect.

In 1837, Birmingham attended a public meeting on wasteland reclamation in Liverpool where he informed those in attendance that his employer had recently converted 100 acres of bog into usable farm land at the cost of £1,421. This land had, by then, been rented out to 20 small occupiers. Bermingham pointed out that a further 500 acres of Clonbrock's wastelands could be cultivated, and urged the same to be done for 'millions of acres of similarly reclaimable bogland in Ireland'.[36] Evidently, drainage and reclamation proceeded apace on the Clonbrock estates; in 1841, a report was read by Captain Waberton at a meeting of the Ballinasloe Agricultural Improvement Society, which stated that 'the bog of Creath [Crith], the property of Lord Clonbrock, where a few years ago he could not get a resting place for his foot while shooting over it, is now yielding luxurious crops and the finest feeding for sheep'.[37] Yet, despite these favourable accounts of Clonbrock's drainage endeavours, verdicts on the effectiveness of these measures were not unanimously positive. According to Caesar Otway, a traveller who passed through east Galway and inquired into the subject in the late 1830s, 'when I asked was the improvement finished, is the red bog become good pasture, meadow, or tillage land, I was told that it was not so yet, and it was more than hinted that his lordship was growing tired of his speculation'.[38] Indeed, Bermingham's replacement as Clonbrock's agent, Charles Filgate, was sceptical of the utility of wasteland reclamation. In 1844, Filgate informed the Devon commission that, while Clonbrock was persisting with reclamation, in his opinion, 'it will not pay. It is the most foolish thing to attempt to reclaim red bog'.[39] Despite criticism of this sort Bermingham always defended the efficacy of the expensive drainage schemes enacted under his supervision, once writing: 'I can fearlessly assert I never laid out one shilling on any drain that has not been amply repaid'.[40]

One of the more notable experiments attempted by Bermingham on Clonbrock's estates, and one that could be appropriately described as the agent's 'pet project', was the application of the principle of 'home colonization' to two of Clonbrock's townlands in south Roscommon: Iskerbane and Castlesampson. Simply put, home colonization was a form of internal migration that involved the reordering of subdivided farms in overpopulated districts by paying a portion of the 'surplus' tenants to relocate to a different part of the estate, which usually consisted of poorer quality land that would then be reclaimed and improved by those tenants. According to Bermingham's account of the scheme, published in 1833, the townland of Iskerbane, which comprised 486 statute acres, had been leased to a middleman who had allowed subdivision and rundale – a 'village system' under which land was held by multiple families in common and divided in portions – to take hold on the land. From an initial division among four tenants, by the early 1820s the townland had been subdivided among 62 families.

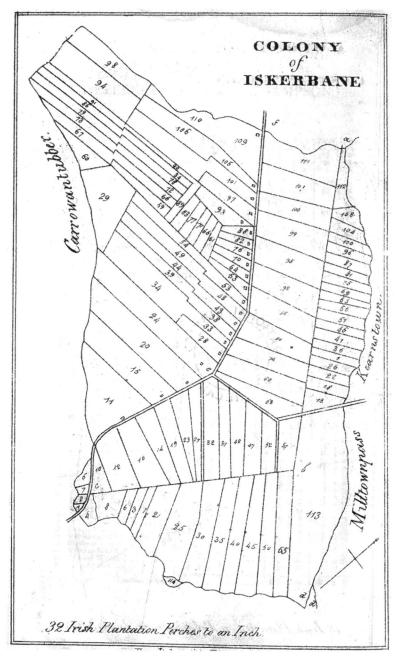

1. Map of Iskerbane, Co. Roscommon.
Source: Thomas Bermingham, *Short narrative of the home colonies of Castle-Sampson and Iskerbane.*

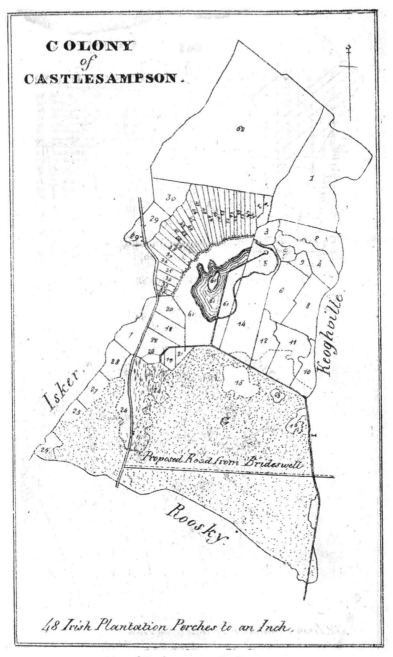

2. Map of Castlesampson, Co. Roscommon.
Source: Thomas Bermingham, *Short narrative of the home colonies of Castle-Sampson and Iskerbane.*

In 1824, this lease expired and the land returned to the possession of Luke Dillon, 2nd Baron Clonbrock, in a disordered state.[41] Following the outbreak of 'great excitement' in the Iskerbane district in 1830, Bermingham suggested home colonization as a way to bring peace and prosperity to the area.[42]

While many commentators called for the consolidation of small Irish holdings into larger farms in the 1820s and 1830s, Bermingham understood that large-scale clearances of small tenants, under-tenants, and cottiers would lead to misery and resistance. As he told the Poor Inquiry, 'the fear of causing an extension of distress has been almost the only cause which has prevented a more rapid junction of farms'.[43] Therefore, instead of advocating a socially disruptive clearance, he proposed a scheme that would not completely depopulate the townland of Iskerbane, but rather make the holdings slightly bigger and end the rundale system there. To achieve this, he aimed to retain 27 of the 'most responsible and best conducted' families and pay the rest to leave.[44] By his own admission, Bermingham took direct inspiration from Belgian agriculture, where small farms proved themselves viable if they were cultivated intensively.[45] According to Bermingham, the implementation of home colonization at Iskerbane 'took place not with a view to making one large farm, but in order to throw a large number of minute holdings into a certain number of 10 acres each' (see fig. 1).[46] Nevertheless, the plan to end rundale and consolidate holdings on this portion of Clonbrock's property hit a road block when 30 of the families deemed 'superabundant' refused to leave, despite an offer of money and their last year's crop for free, and 'although Mr Wilmot Horton's plans for emigration were fully submitted to them'.[47] 'Every anxiety being felt to treat these poor people with kindness', Bermingham wrote in his later account of the scheme, 'it was proposed to take back from a tenant upon a distant part of the estate, some hilly healthy ground, upon which sheep had been fed. This place, called Castlesampson, had the advantage of a very large bog, marked G on the map' (see fig. 2). Clonbrock then offered to relocate the intransigent Iskerbane tenants to Castlesampson, and subsequently assisted them to improve the quality of their new holdings by paying for drainage, the construction of roads, and the erection of cottages.[48]

For their conduct during this episode both Clonbrock and Bermingham were commended by Martin Doyle, the influential Irish agricultural improver and social commentator of the 1820s and 1830s. In an 1835 publication, Doyle wrote as follows: 'instead of "driving out" these human beings, in order to "drive in" sheep, his Lordship allowed Mr Bermingham, his intelligent and humane agent, to locate them on the confines of a bog, where they have a sufficient portion of improvable land'.[49] Bermingham later estimated a total outlay on the scheme of approximately £1,211. Yet, because the rentals for both Iskerbane and Castlesampson had increased since the transplantation had been effected, he believed that the cost would be repaid in the long run, while 'the quiet of the country has been secured, which had been for some time fearfully disturbed'.[50]

As well as overseeing large-scale wasteland reclamation and 'home colonization' schemes, Bermingham also regularly distributed compensation and rent abatements to those tenants who endeavoured to drain their own properties, erected fences, saw to the upkeep of roads, and built houses.[51] Clonbrock was eager not only to enlarge his tenants' holdings, but also to encourage their adoption of improved farming methods by taking heed of the best agronomic advice of the day to obtain greater yields from the land while protecting the productive potential of the soil. During the 1830s and 1840s, proponents of agricultural improvement, such as William Blacker and Martin Doyle, advocated specific advice on the means of improving Irish farming techniques through the introduction of crop rotations, house-feeding livestock, and the popularization of modern agricultural implements among farmers.[52] Both Clonbrock and Bermingham enthusiastically embraced this advice; in effect, they perceived a need for landlords and agents to play a leading role in promoting 'agronomy' – the application of practical experience and scientific insights to agriculture.[53]

One of the means by which Clonbrock and Bermingham tried to promote agricultural improvements was through the introduction of William Blacker's 'green-cropping' system of crop rotations. Blacker was an agent on the properties of the earl of Gosford and Colonel Close in county Armagh, where he demonstrated the utility of alternating corn, oats, barley and potatoes with nitrogen-rich green crops, such as clover and artificial grasses, in the 1820s and early 1830s.[54] At a public meeting of the Ballinasloe Agricultural Improvement Society in 1842, Clonbrock claimed that he 'had long been a disciple of Mr Blacker'.[55] This was evidently true; throughout the 1830s, with Bermingham's aid, he endeavoured to promote Blacker's green-cropping system among his tenants. Charles Clarke, in his report on agriculture in the Kilconnell region of Galway undertaken for the Poor Inquiry in the mid 1830s, noted that 'it is intended to allot the reclaimed bog to the tenants on the Doon townland, for the purpose of growing green crops'.[56] Clonbrock's account books also show that he regularly purchased seeds, lime and ploughs for his tenants' use, which facilitated their adoption of the new farming methods advocated by their landlord and his agent.[57] However, while Bermingham oversaw this expenditure, it was not his responsibility to personally tutor Clonbrock's tenants and labourers on best-practice farming methods; that job fell to the succession of Scottish agriculturalists that Clonbrock employed from the mid 1830s on.[58]

Referring specifically to agents' role in the improvement of agriculture at this time, Martin Doyle advised that 'the care of land property should in no case be committed to persons *utterly* ignorant of rural economy. The knowledge of agriculture, both in theory and details, is as necessary a qualification to the manager of an estate, as acquaintance with the principles and usages of trade, is essential to the merchants'.[59] Bermingham was well versed in the thriving national and international agronomic cultures of his day, including William Blacker's green-cropping system, which he commended in the testimony that he provided to the Poor Inquiry.[60] In this respect, he was representative of the wider concern for agricultural improvement that became common among Irish land agents in the decades before the Great Famine.[61]

Of course, aside from seeing to the purchase of new properties and overseeing improvements such as drainage, home colonization, and green-cropping, Bermingham also had the responsibility of collecting rent. The rentals and estate accounts compiled by Bermingham between 1827 and 1843 have survived and paint a detailed picture of the income and expenditure of the estate during the course of his agency.[62] Throughout the 1830s, the estate generally ran a deficit, due largely to expenditure on permanent improvements and the significant household expenses. Despite this, Bermingham was happy with the investment in projects he approved of – such as home colonization and the reclamation of wasteland – since he believed that those schemes would be remunerating in the long run, but he also endeavoured to cut costs in other areas. In the early 1840s, he embarked on a drive for efficiency, writing that 'the expense of Clonbrock [House] in provisions ... exclusive of the house and what is used in it, certainly costs £1,400 a year for which there appears to be no sensible return and that it never will be cut down unless some decisive measures are adopted such as I adopted last year in the estates'. Bermingham particularly disdained the amount of money that had been spent on forestry, and therefore advised that there should be 'no money to be spent on the woods and nurseries but what is made on them'. He also targeted the demesne farm as a liability, and criticized Henry Wheatley's management of it. Estimating that the operation should be annually generating a £350 profit, Bermingham informed Clonbrock that, if this were not achieved:

I would positively recommend more of the land being let off (so as to stop farming entirely) for sale ... if Wheatley confines himself to the supply of your table with I suppose fifty sheep and twenty kerries and does not think of five cattle for sale this can be acted upon and then perhaps in the end you may be no loser.

Despite his evident desire to cut costs, however, Bermingham was cognisant enough of the social expectations placed on landlords not to take this drive for efficiency too far, exempting the stable yard from his penny-pinching and further stating in his advice to Clonbrock: 'I do not mention servants in house, that forming part of your necessary establishment'.[63] Bermingham clearly understood that a retinue of servants and a certain amount of conspicuous consumption and *noblesse oblige* were an important part of the culture of Ireland's landed class, and a form of patronage through which they asserted their dominance upon the countryside.[64]

Bermingham received ample remuneration for the services that he rendered to Clonbrock, charging an agency fee calculated as a percentage of the expenditure that he oversaw, a fee of nine pence for every pound in the 1830s. Since the accounts were compiled in six month periods – reflecting the payment of rents by most tenants twice a year in May and November – for the extent of his agency one can get a sense of Bermingham's wages from the surviving rent and account books. For his services in the six months from May to November of 1828, for example, Bermingham received an agency fee of £247 12s.[65] As for Bermingham's relationship with his employer, it seems to have been cordial but professional. His surviving letters to Clonbrock generally discuss business affairs, keeping the landlord informed of developments in Galway when he was absent from home, such as when Clonbrock's duties as a representative peer in Westminster's house of lords compelled him to spend time in London.[66]

In one such exchange, upon the opening of the Ballinasloe workhouse in January 1842, Bermingham informed Clonbrock that he

> attended the admission of paupers last Saturday. It is awful the destitution, and the house is not ready to admit all who apply. It is damp & was in my opinion opened too soon. They are very properly sending back to the electoral division the paupers. It will be a great tax unless landlords shall provide for their own paupers out of the house.[67]

Opposition to the opening of workhouses and the passing of the Poor Relief act of 1838 that introduced them was an issue that united Bermingham and Clonbrock.[68] Kevin McKenna has examined this subject in depth, and concluded that they both felt such compulsory, centralized relief would undermine landlord paternalism and, in Bermingham's words, 'snap asunder ties of gratitude and affection'.[69] Despite his initial opposition, however, Bermingham later became a poor law guardian for Ballinasloe union, and gave evidence on poor rate valuations to a parliamentary commission in that capacity in 1842.[70]

Another notable fact about Thomas Bermingham is that he suffered from intermittent illness throughout the 1830s and 1840s. Whether this was the result of a recurring condition or a series of unrelated ailments is unclear, but his correspondence and speeches refer to his periodic indisposition enough to make it worthy of comment. One letter that Bermingham received in May 1833 referred to a recent illness as follows: 'I am very glad to hear that you are rallying and I trust you will find yourself again'.[71] Evidently, his condition persisted or recurred, since he was forced to seek medical treatment in early 1835, and subsequently complimented his doctor for 'curing' him; in his own words, 'having experienced considerable benefit in my health, from the effects of your treatment ... I think it due to you to say so'.[72] However, in 1839, Bermingham apologized for his absence from a meeting on the subject of Irish rail, citing 'an attack of indisposition' as the cause.[73] By 1841 he was unwell again; at a meeting on the topic of Irish infrastructural development that year he remarked that he had ventured from his sick bed to attend. He was still ill the following year, with one correspondent writing that 'I am truly sorry to find you have had such a series of painful illnesses'.[74] In fact, according to a letter that Bermingham wrote in 1855, his health problems were the reason that he left Clonbrock's employment in early 1843.[75]

Despite these ailments, however, Bermingham consistently proved himself a competent manager of his employer's affairs over the course of his 16 year tenure as agent for the Clonbrock estates. In fact, Bermingham earned praise for both his agency and his knowledge of agricultural improvement even outside Ireland, with one English commentator going so far as to say that

> any nobleman or gentleman, who desires information relative to the laying out of his estates, draining of land, and the general improvement of his property, in connexion with that of the peasantry, can scarcely do better than apply to Thomas Bermingham, esq., of Caramana, Kilconnell, Galway. That gentleman has much improved the property of Lord Clonbrock, in Ireland, and obtained a handsome income from a part of the estate of that nobleman, which, before he took it in hand, had been nearly unproductive. His skill and perseverance have not only succeeded in this respect, but his benevolence and success have greatly improved the condition of the peasantry on those estates.[76]

Although Bermingham was by no means faultless, from the perspective of the landed class this commendation was largely deserved, since he proved himself an entrepreneurial land agent with a talent for balancing the often contradictory impulses of improving his employer's economic interests, while simultaneously endeavouring to treat the tenants, cottiers and landless labourers who inhabited the Clonbrock estates with humanity. Bermingham did not spend his time in the 1830s and 1840s occupied solely with his duties as a land agent, however; in these years he also pursued a public career as an advocate of social and economic reform.

2. 'The prophet and the projector': Thomas Bermingham, campaigner and pamphleteer

During the 1830s, while professionally engaged in the management of Lord Clonbrock's estates, Thomas Bermingham also became an active lobbyist and public figure. He achieved this status chiefly through the publication of several pamphlets that suggested schemes for the improvement of agriculture, landlord–tenant relations, and Ireland's transport infrastructure. Moreover, not only did Bermingham write about these subjects, he also participated in committees and societies that pursued these goals. As such, he was responding to and participating in a wider movement for Irish reform. After Daniel O'Connell's successful agitation for Catholic emancipation in 1829, the Whig government in power at Westminster for most of the 1830s, following a policy of 'justice for Ireland', enacted a series of reforms. These included the establishment of a national Board of Education in 1831, the reorganization of the Royal Irish Constabulary, the abolition of the controversial tithe tax, and the introduction of workhouses as a safety net for Ireland's poor.[1] In the midst of this culture of governmental reform there was also an indigenous push for 'improvement', as landlords and agents increasingly took heed of widespread poverty, the supposedly unviable size of tenants' holdings on many estates, the underdeveloped nature of Ireland's transport system, and the inefficient farming practices of the country small farmer and cottier classes.[2]

From his role as an agent, Thomas Bermingham was well acquainted with the myriad problems faced by Irish landlords, tenants, and rural labourers. Demonstrating the social conscience that was apparent in his professional career, he consistently endeavoured to disseminate his insights on Irish problems in the hope that he could spur others to exertion in the areas he identified as requiring improvement. In fact, Bermingham often directly applied his experience on the Clonbrock estate to the wider country, fully confident that his own practices were worthy of emulation. For example, he published an account of his home colonization scheme in 1833, and urged others to adopt the measure whose utility he claimed to have proven on the Clonbrock estate, declaring that 'I tried this with effect, and can pronounce it to be a wholesome process, capable of considerable and almost unlimited extension'.[3] In practice, however, home colonization – though supported by the influential Martin Doyle who deemed the idea 'as worthy of imitation (under similar circumstances), as it is deserving of praise' – appears to have been ignored by most Irish landlords, probably due to its expense, as well as the general reluctance of tenants to give up their holdings.[4]

Furthermore, as Kevin McKenna has pointed out, even on Clonbrock's property the scheme might not have been as successful as Bermingham led the public to believe, with some evictions taking place from Castlesampson and Iskerbane in 1835 and 1838.[5] Nevertheless, home colonization did contribute to a wider push for the consolidation of small holdings and the reclamation of wastelands throughout Ireland during the 1830s and 1840s. In fact, James S. Donnelly has discussed improvement projects undertaken in Cork in the mid-1830s that bear a striking resemblance to Bermingham's scheme, and that might well have been either directly or indirectly influenced by the home colonization experiment undertaken on the Clonbrock estates.[6]

In many respects, Bermingham's public pronouncements were rooted in his experiences as a land agent; his urge for others to apply home colonization to their properties was only one example of this proclivity for him to project improvements that he believed worked on the estates under his supervision onto wider society. As Clonbrock's agent, Bermingham consistently witnessed what he saw as the social and economic benefits that stemmed from the cultivation of paternalism between landlords and tenants, once stating: 'wherever I have found *the tenant cared for by the landlord, he duly appreciates such kindness*'.[7] Consequently, he advised all Irish landlords to uphold their paternalistic 'duties' to their tenantry, and to embark upon improvement projects that would simultaneously provide employment for the poor labourers and cottiers in their localities and benefit themselves. In a sense, Bermingham believed that Irish landlordism should resemble the Clonbrock estates writ large. In pursuit of this end he recommended that 'an estated gentleman ought to expend 20 per cent of the income derived from his estate on its improvement'.[8] As well as drainage and home colonization, he advised that labourers' cottages should be erected and maintained by the landlord, as happened on Clonbrock's properties.[9]

Bermingham also encouraged landlords to assist some of their tenants to emigrate on the basis of his personal experiences with this practice. In his testimony to the Poor Inquiry, he stated his belief that there was a general impulse among the poorer sections of Connacht's peasantry to emigrate, remarking: 'the Clonbrock labourers have told me they would start immediately if they had but £5. This morning a man who has a large family told me he was trying to get off to America, because he feared that if he stayed in Ireland the time might come when he would be turned on the world'.[10] Although Clonbrock did not organize large-scale assisted emigration schemes, he did regularly provide money for a number of his tenants to emigrate during the 1830s and 1840s.[11] Bermingham later claimed that this policy of assisting 'surplus' tenants to emigrate had 'eminently succeeded in the county of Galway, where I was enabled by the landlord to put it in force during a period of sixteen years, whilst administering the Clonbrock estates'.[12] During the Famine, he became even more convinced of the desirability of emigration for Ireland's poor, especially to Canada and Australia. In 1847, he relayed information to the *Western Star* that he had received on the possibilities for employment in Adelaide in the hope that 'means will be afforded by poor law guardians, landed proprietors, and the government, to allow our starving young men and women to take advantage of this information to go out to Australia'.[13]

Although Bermingham prescribed emigration – particularly for landless labourers – as part of his vision of modernization, he did not believe that it alone could or should solve rural Ireland's problems.[14] For the majority of Irish tenants, he advocated the adoption of the new farming methods that were deployed on the Clonbrock estates, which promised to make small holdings both productive and profitable.[15] In the late 1830s and early 1840s, building upon the enthusiasm for agronomy that had been fostered in the preceding decades by 'improvers' including William Blacker, Martin Doyle and Thomas Bermingham, agricultural societies with similar agendas were founded throughout Ireland.[16] In February 1841, for example, progressive members of the landed class founded the Royal Agricultural Improvement Society of Ireland (RAIS) with a view to encouraging agronomy among a greater number of landlords and tenants than had hitherto embraced 'improved' farming techniques.[17] A firm believer in the utility of agricultural improvement, Bermingham donated £10 to the RAIS and sat upon its council in 1841.[18] Additionally, he also gave his backing to one of the RAIS's many affiliated local farming societies: the Ballinasloe Agricultural Improvement Society (BAIS), which was founded in September 1840 and included Lord Clonbrock as one of its vice-presidents.[19] Bermingham's support for these organizations is unsurprising considering his superintendence of agronomic improvements on the Clonbrock estates and his praise for their attendant socioeconomic benefits.

Bermingham maintained that 'whenever the spirit of improvement shall take hold of the minds of our gentry, then, and not till then, will the energies of Ireland be put forth'.[20] The agricultural societies founded throughout Ireland during the 1830s and 1840s were imbued with this 'spirit of improvement', although their success in convincing all Irish landlords to participate and to invest in applying agronomy to their estates appears to have been limited.[21] Nevertheless, the RAIS and BAIS were notable manifestations of the push for self-modernization that characterized a significant number of Irish landlords and their agents in the first half of the 19th century. However, the existence of an impulse for elite-led 'improvement' in this period is often obscured by the Great Famine, which further sullied the already inauspicious reputation of Irish agents and landlords, some of whom had long been working individually, and latterly in a co-ordinated fashion as members of farming societies, for the amelioration of Irish agriculture in the years immediately preceding the catastrophe precipitated by the arrival of potato blight in 1845.[22] Through his participation in agricultural societies, his publications, and his reputation as a 'benevolent' agent on the Clonbrock estates, Bermingham earned a national profile for his views regarding the condition of Ireland's labouring classes. Not only was he included in John Hull's *Philanthropic repertory* in 1841, but John Pitt Kennedy – another Irish land agent and 'improver' with a prominent public profile – also dedicated a book to Bermingham, among others, in recognition of his efforts to encourage social and economic reform.[23]

While Bermingham gained a national reputation for his encouragement of agricultural improvement and the cultivation of paternalistic relations on the estates under his management, the area in which he unquestionably found his niche was in his persistent advocacy of the necessity for the development of Ireland's transport network. In August 1851, during a banquet held to mark the arrival of the first train from Dublin in Galway, Captain Francis Manly Shaw Taylor, the high sheriff of the county, referred to Bermingham as 'the prophet and the projector' of the various infrastructural improvements that had been achieved in Ireland during the previous two decades. Bermingham began this aspect of his career in 1831, when he was co-founder, along with Lord Clonbrock and others, of the Western Railroad and Navigation Company. This short-lived enterprise was formed with the object of soliciting funds for the completion of two projects; the first envisioned the construction of canals to connect Galway with Killala via Lough Corrib, and the second entailed the extension of a railroad from Galway to Loughrea, with the ultimate aim of connecting Galway with Dublin.[24]

Although Bermingham later achieved notoriety for his work lobbying for the diffusion of rail throughout Ireland, he initially focused primarily on obtaining government funding for the improvement of the river Shannon as a means of transport, in conjunction with canals and the introduction of steam-powered vessels on the river. Taking inspiration from a 1794 report, which stated that 'the completing of the navigation of the river Shannon ... would tend effectually to improve and open the home and foreign markets to the produce of more than two millions of acres of land in the heart of the Kingdom', Bermingham called a public meeting on the subject in 1831. At that meeting a report was commissioned, which estimated the improvement of the Shannon and drainage of the adjacent lands would cost approximately £153,000.[25] A constant theme of his writings, Bermingham urged the government to invest in this project not only because it would give isolated western districts easier access to markets, but also because it would provide employment for poor labourers, and thereby bring prosperity that would 'pacify the people' in a region that had long been disturbed by social unrest and the activities of agrarian secret societies. 'Let these very characters (now bad, wild, and disorderly) be set to work', he wrote, 'the best policeman you can have will be the overseer of this work – employ these men by day and you need not watch them at night'.[26] Bermingham considered his efforts in the sphere of inland navigation as a success. In 1841, he remarked at a public meeting that £600,000 had been granted by the government for the improvement of the navigation of the river Shannon, and emphasized the leading role he played in obtaining this sum.[27]

Ever ready to back a new scheme, in the second half of the 1830s Bermingham turned his attention toward campaigning for the introduction of rail into Ireland. He was one of a group of early rail enthusiasts who were motivated to invest in Irish railroads out of a mixture of self-interest and a sense of patriotism. Together, through their creation of numerous rail companies during the 1830s and 1840s, these men generated what Tom Ferris has called an Irish 'railway mania'.[28] Having witnessed the utility of rail on the Clonbrock estates – where moveable rail lines were utilized when carrying out large-scale drainage schemes – Bermingham became convinced that a country-wide railway network was an essential requirement in order for Ireland to modernize.[29] In 1838, he called a meeting that took place in Dublin on 22 November at which the General Irish Railway Committee (GIRC) was formed with the object of bringing private Irish rail companies together to lobby for the government's co-operation with their endeavours to construct railroads throughout Ireland.[30] The GIRC was also intended to protect the interests of the entrepreneurs whose investments in private rail companies were threatened by the establishment of a railway commission in 1836 (known as the Drummond commission) and the publication of its report, which advised the government to construct two main railroads in Ireland.[31] In April 1839, in his capacity as chairman of the GIRC, Bermingham called a meeting of interested parties in London to discuss the prospect of introducing rail into Ireland, and served on the resulting deputation to the lord lieutenant – Lord Morpeth. At the preliminary meeting, held at the Thatched House Tavern, referring to a mooted plan to connect Dublin to Galway with a railroad, Bermingham boldly stated, 'without fear of contradiction, that the running of a line from Dublin to Galway would be attended with great and incalculable advantages to both kingdoms, by forming a more direct communication with America'. He also maintained that by completing a line similar to one he knew of in Sweden 'so might Ireland command a vast trade from Russia by the Baltic with America'.[32]

To achieve the construction of such a railroad from Dublin to Galway, Bermingham initially placed his faith in private enterprise, since he believed that Irish and British capitalists would be eager to invest in Irish rail companies. The meeting went against him on this point, however, with a majority of the attendees voting in favour of soliciting the state to complete three main rail lines, projected to extend north, south, and west from Dublin. This conclusion stemmed from the widespread belief that English capitalists were generally uninterested in the opportunity of funding Irish rail companies and that there was a dearth of venture capital within Ireland for rail construction projects. One attendee, Ashton Yeats, stated at the Thatched House Tavern meeting:

I have had occasion to make some inquiries in the City as to the practicability of procuring advances from private capitalists for railways in Ireland, and I can take it upon me to state that no considerable sum could be obtained in that quarter for any such purpose. If, therefore, any lines of railway are to be executed in that country, they must be executed either by the State or by Irish capitalists, and the latter alternative I look upon as altogether visionary.[33]

The meeting formed a deputation, on which Bermingham served, which met Lord Morpeth on 3 May 1839 to present their petition for the government to consider investing in Irish rail.[34]

Bermingham's conduct during this episode caused a minor controversy, since he had attended the meetings on rail at the Thatched House Tavern and the subsequent interview with Lord Morpeth as a representative of private interests. A special meeting of the GIRC on 10 May 1839 repudiated Bermingham's acquiescence to the resolution for state-executed rail construction, rather than the state loans for private companies that they had desired; as they saw it, Bermingham's consent was taken as 'official abandonment of the rights of the private enterprise by one authorized to do so'.[35] Bermingham publicly defend himself from these accusations, responding that

> I advocated the cause of private enterprise so long as there was a chance of its success; but finding the opinion strongly against it, and having from Lord Morpeth the determination that the Government would not lend money to private parties, and likewise having the opinion of the majority of the Irish members ... that it should be left in the hands of the Government, I determined not to oppose the project of the government executing the three trunk lines impartially to the north, south, and west, but I did not pledge any other party to my opinion, but spoke for myself alone.[36]

While it was true that – according to the account of the meeting with the lord lieutenant that he subsequently published – Bermingham did emphasize that he only spoke for himself, it is understandable that his statement that 'I would be glad to support the Government in their intentions to complete the lines, and would endeavour to persuade those whom I now represent to do the same', would have rankled with those individuals who wished to keep the government out of what they saw as the realm of private enterprise.[37]

Thus, although Bermingham represented private interests in his capacity as chairman of the GIRC, he soon became convinced that Ashton Yeats was correct in his calculations that private enterprise alone would not raise the funds to introduce rail into Ireland. In a letter dated 25 May 1839, responding to the criticism that he strayed beyond the remit imposed upon him as a representative of the GIRC, he elaborated on the reasons why his opinion was 'now decidedly in favour of Government's construction of the three trunk lines, north, south, and west, impartially'.[38] Foremost among the reasons he gave for his change of opinion was the example of Belgian rail, where lines were constructed by the state and, according to evidence furnished by Bermingham, proved to be more efficient than English private rail lines.[39] Later, in 1841, Bermingham explained that he had 'became a thorough convert to the principle, that if an extended system of railroads (which the wants of Ireland demanded) were ever to be made, it must be by the *State*', and further affirmed that his experience of Belgian rail when he visited there in 1837 convinced him that state-constructed rail could be efficient, safe, and profitable.[40] He calculated that the completion of a line from Dublin to Galway – via Mullingar, Athlone, and Ballinasloe – necessitated £100,000, which he hoped the government would provide, writing in December 1841: 'I think we are quite entitled to ask government, through the medium of Public Works, for a free grant of two-fifths of this sum, and for the loan of the remainder at five per cent'.[41]

Despite coming to believe that the government should fund, or partially fund, the construction of three trunk lines in Ireland, Bermingham nevertheless also still envisioned an important role for private companies in the construction and operation of Irish railroads. He argued that

> if government shall persevere in its intention of making Irish railways, I conclude it must have them executed by contract, so that here private enterprise must aid in their formation; again after the rail road is open Government must let the carrying also by the tender, and here again private enterprise must help them.[42]

Bermingham's support for the private Irish rail companies that were founded during the 1840s, in a second phase of 'railway mania' that gripped the country after it became clear that the government did not intend to construct an Irish rail network, is therefore unsurprising. Foremost among these companies was the Great Southern and Western Railroad of Ireland (GSWR), which projected a line from Dublin to Cork and another from Dublin to Galway. However, when the GSWR decided to abandon their plan for a line to Connacht there was a split in the organization and a rival company, the Midland Great Western Railroad of Ireland (MGWR), was formed with a view toward completing a line to Galway.[43] By 1847, the MGWR's privately funded railroad to Mullingar was underway and the company had obtained parliamentary approval for their planned extension to Galway, via Athlone; but it did not have the necessary capital to extend the line as envisioned. At this point, Bermingham threw his support behind the MGWR. In October 1847, the *Galway Vindicator* reported that a deputation of the directors of this company arrived in Ballinasloe accompanied by Thomas Bermingham, who submitted a detailed plan on behalf of the company for the consideration of the Ballinasloe poor law union's board of guardians. Under the provisions of this plan:

the directors propose to purchase the land from the head-landlords ... and
pay the occupying tenants in cash, and thus put the Board of Guardians in
possession of the land for the railway and in case the Board of Guardians
will employ those who are to get outdoor relief in executing the earth
works ... the directors will send them engineers and officers to see the
work properly executed, and will bind the Company to take the line.[44]

As well as supporting the MGWR's initiative by representing them in their
dealings with western poor law unions in this manner, Bermingham also
continued to call for the government to partially fund rail lines that private
companies, such as the MGWR, would execute.[45]

However, in the free trade climate that was ascendant in early-Victorian
England, efforts to secure either state-executed rail lines or state loans to
fund Irish rail companies were unpopular at Westminster, with multiple
parliamentary bills for this purpose failing during the 1840s. Nevertheless,
Bermingham continued to lobby for the introduction of rail, although he
was forced to resign as chairman of the GIRC, reputedly due to illness.[46] He
appears to have sincerely believed that 'the amelioration of our fisheries, the
improvement of our waste lands, the introduction of new manufactures, and
the renewal of the flax trade and the coarse linen and woollen trade will date
from the completion of our railroad from sea to sea'.[47] Bermingham's campaign
was incessant. In 1848, at a public meeting in Galway, he acknowledged that
he might have been annoying people by speaking so often about the topic, 'yet
speak he would, until he succeeded in it. It was just the same way some years ago,
when he was endeavouring to obtain the improvement of the river Shannon'.[48]
In the midst of the Famine, Bermingham believed that the construction of
railroads would be of even greater benefit to the country, since it would provide
employment for the starving population and simultaneously bring manifold
long-term benefits to the country.[49] During 'Black '47', for example, he wrote

> circumstanced as Ireland is at present, it is essential to the salvation of
> that country that Government should be prepared to aid such companies
> and private parties by loans of money to a certain extent, and thereby
> encourage the capitalist to supply the principal part of the funds necessary
> to carry out the various undertakings.[50]

This argument was heeded by some politicians, such as Lord George
Benthnick, who introduced an unsuccessful Irish railway bill at Westminster
in 1847 that proposed a government loan of £16 million to private companies
in order to extend rail and provide employment in famine-stricken Ireland.
Thomas Redington, under-secretary at Dublin castle, also proposed a similarly
unsuccessful plan for government-backed Irish rail in 1848.[51] These initiatives
failed chiefly because the state was unwilling to trespass on what was widely

seen as the domain of free enterprise.[52] However, by 1849, spurred on by the persistence of famine in Ireland, the prime minister, Lord John Russell, became more open to the idea of the state lending money to Irish railway companies with a view toward creating employment for starving labourers. Bermingham was finally on the cusp of a long-held ambition; 'this is the moment', he remarked in a March 1849 letter, 'with a pull, a strong pull and a pull together, let us employ our famishing poor in shoving the railroad from Mullingar to Galway'. By June, Bermingham's ambition was fulfilled. He wrote to the editor of the *Tuam Herald* about the 'glorious news' that the chancellor of the exchequer had announced that £500,000 was to be loaned to the MGWR in order to facilitate the completion of their railroad between Dublin and Galway.[53] The resulting construction of the MGWR's extension line from Mullingar to Galway began in August 1849 and was officially completed on 21 July 1851, with the first train arriving in Galway on that day to huge celebrations.[54]

Bermingham saw the MGWR's railway line as his crowning achievement. In an 1855 public letter to John Carr, a Clonbrock tenant, he wrote:

the railroad which you know I initiated, and long worked for, is a fact. Markets, which were before beyond your reach, are now, I may say, at hand. Make use of this engine at your door. Fill its trucks with fresh butter, meat, poultry; with the produce from your profitable soil; take advantage of this new element of power which your fathers never dreamt of.[55]

It is understandable that Bermingham felt the need to remind people of his central role in ensuring that the rail line extended into the west, since much credit for the achievement was given to Anthony O'Flaherty, MP for Galway, and Father Peter Daly.[56] Bermingham had certainly played a leading role for much longer than these relative latecomers, as a proponent of Irish rail from as early as 1831 when he forwarded the idea to form a company to build a line from Galway to Loughrea, as chairman of the GIRC, and through his many pamphlets on the subject over the course of nearly two decades. Recognizing the importance of modern transport in ensuring access to markets, he used the skills and contacts he had cultivated in his earlier endeavours for the improvement of the river Shannon to form committees and lobby for the introduction of rail lines, partially funded by the government and executed by private companies.

While much credit was given to others for ensuring the successful extension of rail to Galway in the early 1850s, Bermingham's role was not forgotten. Aside from the recognition he received at the County Club's celebration to mark the arrival of the first train in Galway, a committee was also formed in early 1852 with a view toward reimbursing him for the money that he had expended in publishing pamphlets on the topic of infrastructural improvement and on commissioning reports and surveys, all of which paved the way for the success of companies like the MGWR and GSWR. According to the estimates of this committee

it appears he [Bermingham] has expended, out of his own private
resources, on the preliminaries of several works now executed, or in
course of execution in the west of Ireland a sum exceeding £3,000
sterling. The prospectus of the committee states that his expenditure in
his long and unceasing effort of turning public opinion in favour of the
Galway Railway, amounts to £1,000.[57]

Such considerable expenditure proves Bermingham's dedication to the cause of
infrastructural improvement over the course of two decades, and demonstrates
that he was not only a 'prophet and a projector', but also a patron of these
modernizing schemes.

The completion of the MGWR's rail line to Galway did not end
Bermingham's interest in transport matters, however, for he soon turned his
attention to the next logical step: crossing the Atlantic. During the 1850s, he
vociferously backed the mooted plan to establish Galway as an official packet
station that could potentially become the focus of the United Kingdom's trade
and communications with North America. Bermingham had long believed
that the introduction of an Irish rail network would naturally lead to Ireland's
increased prominence in British trade with the United States and Canada. In
1845, for example, he had optimistically predicted that when a rail line reached
Galway, 'that moment vessels will be prepared fitted up on the principle of the
Screw Propellor, to navigate between Galway and New York'.[58] Bermingham
was not the only person to hold such hopes, for it was believed locally at the
time that rail 'would open to Galway the traffic of Scotland and the North,
and, joined with steam communication with America, would operate in a few
brief years to elevate the "ancient citie" to a position of commercial greatness'.[59]
Interestingly, this opinion was not confined to the Galway region and cannot
therefore be attributed to mere local boosterism. In his *Thoughts on Ireland*,
Camillo Cavour – himself a well-known Italian 'improver' – also supported the
idea that

> if one of those marvellous lines crossed the island from east to west,
> placing St George's Channel in prompt communication with the western
> shore washed by the Atlantic; if the distance which separates the walls
> of Dublin from the harbours of Connaught could be traversed in eight
> hours, Ireland would of necessity become the highway between the two
> hemispheres.[60]

A packet station and steam communication between Galway harbour
and North America might well have fulfilled these expectations. In 1846,
Bermingham had written: 'of what national importance must the west of
Ireland become; what an enormous amount of good would flow to the
commerce of England, by having these great ports fitted to receive vessels, which

otherwise might be lost, as constantly happens when going around the island.'[61]
In 1851, with a new railroad connecting Galway with Dublin and improvements
undertaken on Galway harbour, Bermingham backed a push for raising funds
to buy a line of steamers in order to give Galway an edge in the competition
to become an officially sanctioned packet station to America, noting that 'the
company that first starts the race must win'.[62] Halting endeavours were pursued
in this sphere throughout the 1850s. In June 1850, the MGWR contributed to
the charter of a steam ship called the *Viceroy* that sailed from Galway to New
York with a view toward proving the expediency of such a route; however,
the vessel was tragically lost at sea on the return journey.[63] An enterprise called
the New York and Galway Steamship Company was also established in 1851,
but soon folded.[64] It was not until 1858, with the backing of the Manchester
industrialist, John Orrell Lever, and his foundation of the 'Galway Line', that
the region made tangible progress in establishing a potentially viable steamship transport route with North America. However, Galway's prospective
emergence as a port of importance in world trade proved largely illusory. The
Galway Line obtained a valuable official postal contract in 1859, but this was
revoked in 1861. The company subsequently encountered financial difficulties,
and Bermingham's predictions that Galway would become a hub of Euro-
American trade never came to pass.[65]

While it might seem that Bermingham jumped from one transport scheme
to another between the 1830s and 1850s, it is clear from his speeches, letters, and
pamphlets that – although his focus switched from inland navigation, to rail, to
a packet station for Galway – from the outset, he envisioned the introduction
of a modern transport network for Ireland that would elevate the country's
importance in international trade. He mentioned rail along with his push for
the improvement of the river Shannon in the early 1830s; he talked about the
idea for a Galway packet station while focused on the introduction of rail; and
he kept a close eye on the improvement of Galway harbour during the 1840s and
1850s.[66]

These efforts in the sphere of infrastructural improvement went some
way toward combatting the widespread international perception that 19th-
century Ireland was a 'backward' country. Complaining about the state of Irish
infrastructure in 1843, the English economist Nassau Senior wrote that 'Ireland
is not on the road to any other place; and the greater part of it is not, at present,
an inviting country to travel in. There are scarcely any railroads ... Until it has
been greatly altered, nothing but necessity will make it frequented by those who
belong to happier countries'.[67]

Bermingham and his fellow lobbyists for Irish rail and for steam-
communication with North America had attempted to remedy this situation,
and to place Ireland not only on the 'road to somewhere', but ambitiously
aimed to make the country a highway for the transport of passengers and goods
between the United Kingdom and the United States, and even between the

whole of Europe and North America. Bermingham's ambition was such that, in 1841, while urging the adoption of his plan for government-backed rail in a letter to the people of Connacht, he looked forward to the completion of his vision, which would 'make Galway a safe and excellent port, and be the certain means of at no distant day bringing the greater part, if not the entire communication between the Continent of Europe and the States of America and the Canadas through their counties'.[68] For an extended moment in the 1850s, with the rejuvenation of Ireland's agricultural economy after the Famine, the completion of the Dublin–Galway railroad, the improvement of Galway harbour, and the foundation of the Galway Line, such optimism can be easily understood.

Time was to prove that, unfortunately for Galway's high hopes, it would not attain the position of prominence in the Atlantic nexus of world trade that Bermingham had prophesied. His former employer, Lord Clonbrock, was nearer the mark in espousing a more pessimistic view on Galway's chances of usurping Liverpool's dominance as the most prominent port in the United Kingdom. Though a supporter of Irish infrastructural improvements and a prominent investor in the MGWR, Clonbrock did not believe that the amelioration of Irish infrastructure would automatically elevate Galway to a position of pre-eminence in world trade.[69] Responding to the idea of a tax on landed proprietors to pay for the erection of a break-water at the city's harbour in 1861, he explained his opposition as follows:

> I believe that a harbour of refuge at Galway would be the means of preserving to a large extent both life and property. I believe also that maintenance of Galway as an American Packet Station is a National object worthy of National support. But you must allow me to add my doubts that the erection of a break-water at Galway must, as a commercial enterprise, be necessarily reproductive. A port does not make trade, though trade makes a port. The manufacturing districts of England have made Liverpool, naturally the worst of all harbours, the first of all ports, while Falmouth, the finest of all English harbours, for many years the English packet station for all parts of the world, is as a trading post of small importance. Many years must elapse (if ever such a time should arrive) before the trade of Galway would be such as to enable the Port Revenues to pay the interest of the money necessary for the execution of the proposed works ... I feel quite sure that liability on the County will be by no means a 'shadow' but a sad reality, and which we shall never be able to remove.[70]

While Clonbrock had been prepared to invest in projects that he considered remunerating, such as the MGWR, he was evidently sceptical that Galway could usurp English ports in commanding British trade with North America, and was therefore unwilling to submit to taxation in pursuit of what he believed was an unattainable goal. Considering the ignominious fortunes of the Galway Line between 1858 and 1861, Clonbrock could be forgiven for his pessimistic appraisal of the situation. Galway's apparent moment of rejuvenation had come and gone; it would never achieve the position of prominence in national and international trade that it had seemed on the cusp of gaining during the 1850s.

Nevertheless, the infrastructural improvement projects that Bermingham had contributed to were by no means redundant. Thus, when he was commended by the chairman of an 1851 meeting of the County Club in Galway as 'the prophet and the projector of those great improvements which are destined to make Galway one of the foremost towns in the kingdom', the credit was largely warranted.[71] Bermingham had truly taken the lead in agitating for Irish infrastructural development during the previous two decades. The fact that those improvements did not make Galway the fulcrum of Euro-American transport and trade may have rendered Bermingham a false prophet in the eyes of some, but the construction of a rail network and the improvement of the Shannon as a navigable river were still of considerable benefit to Ireland. In practice, the completion of these projects facilitated the quicker and cheaper transport of Irish manufactured goods and agricultural produce – especially livestock in the post-Famine era – to British markets, particularly when allied with the introduction of steamships on the Irish sea.[72] As a result, Ireland did benefit from Bermingham's efforts to prominently situate the country in transatlantic trade routes, which were simultaneously successful in their corollary function: the provision of Irish farmers and manufacturers with more expedient access to local and British markets.

3. 'A fallen politician': Bermingham and the corn law controversy of 1841

In 1841, Thomas Bermingham became embroiled in a controversy that threatened his professional career as Lord Clonbrock's land agent. In late May of that year he attended a meeting in Loughrea, Co. Galway, on the subject of the corn laws, at which he was criticized for his stance on the issue. The resulting coverage of the incident saw him condemned in conservative newspapers, some of which publicly called for his dismissal from his job as Clonbrock's agent. The events of the Loughrea corn law meeting and its subsequent reporting in the press provide an interesting perspective on Bermingham's politics, as well as an insight into the expectations and social conventions that influenced the behaviour of land agents in 19th-century Ireland.

By 1841, Bermingham had earned himself a national reputation for his efforts in the cause of Irish infrastructural improvement, while he was also held in high esteem for his agency of the Clonbrock estates in counties Galway and Roscommon. Generally, Bermingham refrained from taking a public stance on politics, as befitted his agenda to solicit cross-partisan support for his various improvement schemes. Nevertheless, his pamphlets betray an unmistakable affinity for the Whig party, especially evident in his admiration for Thomas Drummond, the reforming Whig under-secretary stationed at Dublin castle in the latter half of the 1830s.[1] Bermingham did not agree with the Whig leadership on all issues, however. He argued against the introduction of workhouses into Ireland under the Poor Law act of 1838, and he also supported the principle of protection for the United Kingdom's tillage farmers that was contrary to the shift toward an acceptance of free trade in British politics, especially among the Whigs. British industrialization – fuelled largely by textile manufacturing in northern England – saw the increasing ascendency of free trade ideals at Westminster in the 1830s and 1840s. In this context, the issue of the corn laws became a battle ground between the United Kingdom's landed aristocracy and its newer industrial interests and rising middle class.

Introduced at the end of the Napoleonic wars in 1815, the corn laws afforded protection to British and Irish tillage farmers by imposing tariffs and restrictions on the United Kingdom's imports of foreign grain. However, in a climate where the *laissez-faire* ideas of classical political economists such as Adam Smith and David Ricardo gained prominence as England sought to penetrate the markets of rival empires and states as the 19th century advanced, this protectionism was assailed. The Anti-Corn Law League, founded by Richard Cobden in 1839, demanded a repeal of the corn laws so that the working classes of Britain's industrial cities, as well as labourers in rural districts, could access cheaper bread.[2] The Conservative party – bastion of the pan-United Kingdom landed interest – supported the retention of the corn laws. Most Irish landlords, even prominent Whig landowners such as Thomas Redington of Clarinbridge, Co. Galway, opposed any change in the protectionist measures from which they ultimately benefited through the rents that they charged those of their tenants who relied on tillage farming.[3]

Thomas Bermingham was of the same opinion until 1841. In 1839, he marshalled support in Galway for a petition to parliament that opposed mooted plans to alter the corn laws. At a public meeting on the issue in February of the same year, Clonbrock was called upon to introduce this pro-corn law petition into the house of lords; however, the following month, the document, which had gathered 4,000 signatures with Bermingham's help, was reportedly lost in the post![4] Again in 1840, Bermingham attended a meeting on the issue of the corn laws in Galway where he 'at very considerable length, advocated the necessity of adhering to the present system, as a change in the corn laws would destroy the prospects of the agriculturist, and reduce Ireland to a state of poverty and destitution'. At this meeting, Bermingham again proposed the adoption of a petition to that effect for submission to parliament.[5]

However, in 1841, Bermingham changed his stance on the issue. In May of that year he published a pamphlet, titled *A letter on the corn laws*, which argued for the necessity not to repeal the corn laws but to alter them. As they stood, the tariffs were set on a sliding scale, whereby in seasons with low yields of British and Irish grain the small quantity was counterbalanced by remunerative prices supported by high tariffs on imports of foreign grain. Bermingham advocated an alternative system of protection for grain produced within the United Kingdom under which this sliding scale would be replaced by a fixed rate that would allow tillage products to be imported from abroad once the price of British and Irish grain rose above 30*s.* per 20 stone barrel.[6] In this respect, he had evidently been converted to the opinion of William Blacker, a fellow Irish land agent and 'improver', who had elaborated on the virtues of a fixed duty on foreign corn in an 1836 publication.[7] Advocating a similar fixed rate of protection in his own pamphlet, dated 22 May 1841, Berminham wrote: 'If our landlords would but consider, as they ought, the dreadful distress which their poorer tenants encounter in dear years; the enormous sums they run in debt to raise provisions from meal-mongers on time, they would pause before they sought to exclude corn in such seasons'.[8]

On 25 May 1841, William Le Poer Trench, 3rd earl of Clancarty – a prominent landowner, president of the Ballinasloe Agricultural Improvement Society, and a close personal friend of Lord Clonbrock's – held a public meeting in Loughrea, Co. Galway, in support of his petition that the corn laws remain unaltered. Bermingham refused to sign this petition, but attended the meeting nevertheless. What followed was subsequently reported in different ways in the press depending on their stance on the corn laws. Bermingham apparently attended the event, which took place in Loughrea court house, with the intention of observing the proceedings but not participating. The meeting took place against a backdrop of tensions in the town that were sparked by the issue; that morning, for example, a placard appeared on the streets that read: 'Cheap bread or ultimate starvation. Men of Loughrea, be at your post to-day, and convince the grinding aristocracy of this county, by your undivided confidence in the present government, that you shall have no Corn Law! ... Let cheap bread be your motto'.[9]

Inside the packed courthouse, Clancarty spoke at length about the necessity of maintaining the corn laws unaltered, and proposed the adoption of a petition to that effect. In the midst of this speech, Clancarty referred to the presence of Thomas Bermingham, a man who had been a staunch advocate of the principle of unaltered corn laws over the previous two years but who had refused to sign his latest petition. Clancarty also referred to Bermingham's efforts to introduce rail into Ireland, and hinted that his recent about-turn on the issue of the corn laws might have been a political ploy intended to curry favour with the Whig government in power at the time. To be sure, it was certainly suspicious that Bermingham's move from an ardent faith in the availability of private capital to fund the expansion of railroads in Ireland to a belief in the necessity for state intervention to achieve this aim corresponded with his change of opinion with regard to the corn laws. Clancarty invited Bermingham to explain his motives to the assembled audience.[10] Bermingham had little choice but to reply. Upon ascending the stage he was met with derision from some members of the crowd, since, according to the anti-corn law Tuam Herald, it had been packed with 'the serfs of Garbally [Clancarty's big house] ... trained and mustered for the demonstration'.[11] It took the intercession of Lord Clancarty and the local priest to quell the tumult.

Bermingham proceeded to admit that he had previously supported the retention of the Corn Laws as they stood, and explained: 'I am now, as then, for ample "protection"; but I beg to state in my own defence that I could not sign the requisition for the present meeting ... I objected ... because I am firmly convinced some alteration is necessary'. The reasons he gave for this change of opinion were his recent witness of hunger and deprivations caused by localized crop failures, combined with the influence of a report on European agriculture from which he learned that 'it is not so easy as people imagined to get corn from abroad; in many parts of Poland it is stored in caves, and it is only a very high price in England that can draw it forth'. On these grounds, Bermingham challenged Clancarty: 'does the noble lord mean to say that the starvation which I have witnessed from high prices of those sad years is to have no effect on me and others?'[12] Bermingham contended that, in seasons of plenty, the present law was suitable, but in seasons of scarcity the sliding-scale corn laws failed to provide cheap food for the people. As a result, he reiterated his proposal for a fixed duty that would allow for the importation of foreign grain only when the price of Irish corn rose above 30*s.* per 20 stone barrel.[13] Bermingham finished his speech, the meeting continued, and Clancarty's motion in support of his petition to retain the existing system of sliding-scale corn laws was put to a vote. It was defeated. What followed was a hail of abuse for Bermingham from conservative newspapers.

In the controversy that followed, contrasting reports of the Loughrea corn law meeting were published in the local and national press. The local anti-corn law newspaper – the *Tuam Herald* – welcomed the rejection of Clancarty's petition and hailed

> the accession of Mr Bermingham, the agent of an excellent landlord, though a Tory peer, Lord Clonbrock, as a most valuable proof of the light in which this question is regarded by all not the stultified partizans of a place-hunting clique reckless alike of means and ends, so that they may be enabled to fatten on the vitals of the country.[14]

On the other side of the political divide, the conservative *Dublin Evening Mail* and *Galway Weekly Advertiser* condemned the results of the meeting, and Bermingham's participation in particular. The former wrote that 'the agricultural interests of the county was on this occasion overruled by the nonsense and clamour of the populace and their leaders', while 'the same elements of popular opinion would pass a vote of confidence in a broom-stick, if Dr MacHale [the Catholic Archbishop of Tuam] had set it up'.[15] The latter stated that 'a *silly* exhibition he [Bermingham] made there', while emphasizing the heckles he received from the crowd, such as the cries of 'shut your mouth, we know you well, railway, none of your blarney', that interrupted him.[16]

The main complaint of these conservative organs was that, in the absence of Lord Clonbrock, who supported the retention of the existing sliding-scale corn laws, Bermingham was considered by many of those present to be speaking for his employer. According to the *Galway Weekly Advertiser* this clarification might have changed the result of the meeting, since it noted that Clonbrock

> from the Roman Catholics, gets credit for extreme moderation in religion and politics – but anything emanating from Garbally is supposed to be but high Tory, and many refrained from joining the corn law ranks under the erroneous impression that Lord Clancarty got up the meeting for party purposes … Lord Clonbrock's name, under those circumstances, would, we re-assert, influence the opinions of very many Roman Catholics. We, therefore, think Mr Bermingham, now a *fallen* politician, did not deal with him in a spirit of fair play.[17]

Because of this perceived transgression, the *Evening Mail* called for Bermingham's dismissal as Clonbrock's agent, writing in an editorial that 'if he [Clonbrock] continues to counteract himself and his principles, by retaining Mr Bermingham in his service, he will not only disappoint his friends, and disserve the cause which he has at heart, but be responsible for the mischiefs that may arise from such pernicious agency'.[18]

Much of this criticism was unfair to Bermingham, who stated at the meeting in question that Clonbrock's stance on the corn laws was in unison with that of Clancarty, and also remarked that his employer 'entertains a very poor opinion indeed of my politics, and I have never conceded them – I see no reason why I should do so'.[19] Therefore, in response to the *Evening Mail*'s calls for his dismissal, Bermingham wrote to the editor to defend himself. He stated that

> the experience I have had in the last two years, of the suffering of the poorer classes, from the high price of provisions, made me feel that I could not consciously continue my support to a system which put so heavy a duty on foreign corn, after the price exceeded what I considered a fair remuneration for farmers in ordinary seasons.

In addition, Bermingham emphasized that he had made a distinction between his own views and those of Clonbrock when he spoke in Loughrea. He also mentioned, in his defence, that he had refrained from backing a resolution that pledged support to the Whig government, out of respect to Clonbrock.[20] The *Evening Mail* refused to back down however, since it maintained that Bermingham had no business attending the meeting 'if he were not resolved to defend his employer', since this was his 'duty as an agent of the landed interest'. Although they acknowledged that he made a distinction between his own views and Clonbrock's, they believed 'that disclaimer was not likely to affect the understanding of the ignorant rabble whom he addressed'.[21] The paper even went so far as to question Lord Clonbrock's conservative credentials on the basis of the actions of his agent, announcing: 'we can assure his Lordship that until he takes up some declaratory of his sense of the question, so as to leave no doubt as to the approval or disapprobation of his agent's conduct, the question will not cease to be asked: is Lord Clonbrock a Corn Law repealer?'[22]

Clonbrock had evidently missed the Loughrea corn law meeting because of the death of his grandmother, Letitia Dillon, in London, since this death was reported in the press at roughly the same time.[23] Despite dealing with this bereavement, Clonbrock was forced to respond to the controversy sparked by his agent. 'Perceiving in the *Evening Mail* of yesterday that you have thought it proper to ask, "is Lord Clonbrock a Corn Law repealer?"' he wrote in an open letter to the editor, 'I think it due to myself to answer my question most distinctly in the negative'. Referring to the controversy that had arisen over Bermingham's conduct, he added 'without expressing any opinion as to the part taken by my agent ... I must say that he knew his opinions differed from mine, and that he distinctly stated so to the meeting; adding that he did not appear there as my representative'.²⁴ Meanwhile, the *Tuam Herald* defended Bermingham from the 'calumnies' of the 'Orange press' and lauded Clonbrock for his magnanimity; as they saw it:

> for the dreadful crime of honestly avowing his opinions he [Bermingham] is marked out as a victim – and had Lord Clonbrock been as weak as others were malicious, vengeance would have been wreaked upon an honest man for daring to give utterance to his sentiments; but his Lordship, though a conservative, is still a gentleman.²⁵

Although Lord Clonbrock did not heed the calls for Bermingham's dismissal, he would surely have been displeased with his agent for so publicly embarrassing him, given that, as the *Dublin Evening Mail* believed was the case:

> his Lordship's compeers – the nobility, gentry, and other agricultural classes of this great county – will not be satisfied with him for allowing the influence and example of his very considerable estate to be a drawback upon any exertions that they can make for sustaining the constitution, and rescuing their country from radical thraldom.²⁶

In the long run, however, the episode does not appear to have permanently soured the relationship between Clonbrock and his chief agent. While Bermingham retired from Clonbrock's employment less than two years later, this was reportedly due to illness.²⁷ Furthermore, Clonbrock acted as treasurer to the committee, formed in 1852, which solicited donations to reimburse Bermingham for his considerable expenditure on the promotion of Irish infrastructural improvement.²⁸ It does not seem, therefore, that the corn law controversy led to a permanent schism between Bermingham and Clonbrock.

Nevertheless, the incident is a telling example of the grey area that land agents occupied in 19th-century Ireland. They could only act as independent political players to a limited extent, since they were widely considered to have been projections of the landlord's power. While Bermingham's role as a land agent provided him with the requisite wealth, experience, and social stature to formulate, comment on, and participate in various improvement schemes, he was evidently considered to have strayed beyond his remit on this occasion. In doing so his public activism contradicted what the *Dublin Evening Mail* saw as his first 'duty' as a land agent, convincing them of the necessity for landlords to ensure 'a complete harmony of sentiment and conduct between themselves and their agents'.²⁹ Thus, it was only when Bermingham left Clonbrock's employment in 1843 that he became more explicitly political in his public declarations.

4. Bermingham after Clonbrock

Charles Filgate replaced Thomas Bermingham as Lord Clonbrock's land agent in February 1843, but Bermingham had no intention of a quiet retirement. As we have seen, during the 1840s and 1850s, he continued to campaign for the development of Irish rail and its extension into Connacht, as well as backing the establishment of Galway as a packet-station for North American transport and trade. Freed from the constraints of his professional responsibilities from February 1843 on, Bermingham also became distinctly more political in his public pronouncements. The same year that he left Clonbrock's employment, in a letter to the prime minister of the day, Sir Robert Peel, Bermingham openly threatened to support the Repeal movement – which was then gathering momentum under the leadership of Daniel O'Connell – if something were not done by the government to ameliorate conditions in Ireland. He wrote, 'unless there be speedily a change, most certainly of measures, moderate men, who, like myself, are attached to the connexion of the countries, and desirous of a real union between them, may, in despair, though unwillingly, be found, perhaps at no distant day, in the ranks of the repealers'.[1] Considering that Bermingham caused a minor controversy by merely giving utterance to his views on an alteration of the corn laws in 1841, such a statement could never have been made publicly when he was in Clonbrock's employment, since it would have reflected badly upon his employer who was a prominent member of the Conservative party and a staunch unionist. Nor could Bermingham feasibly have backed the idea of government regulation of landlord–tenant relations as he also did during the 1840s.

In 1846, spurred by the onset of the Great Famine, Bermingham addressed a publication to the Whig prime minister, Lord John Russell. In it he argued that, because only a minority of landlords were fulfilling their responsibilities, it was necessary for the duties and rights of landlords and tenants to be established in law, since 'the business of legislation is to induce or even force those who act upon a different principle to follow the example set by these good landlords, or make them pay the penalty of their neglect'.[2] Bermingham's experience as an agent had evidently convinced him that, while Lord Clonbrock and other Irish landowners acted in what he considered an admirable manner in the running of their estates, there were some, 'I fear I must say *many*, who look merely to the produce of the estate as a matter of pounds, shillings and pence, totally unmindful of the various duties which are required at the hand of the landlord'. As a result, he argued: 'surely then, some law is necessary (when the commands of God and the duties enjoined by the Christian religion are not found sufficient), to force such landlords to act in a fair spirit by the tenants placed under their care'.[3] Specifically, Bermingham supported the idea that tenants should be legally guaranteed compensation for the improvements they made on their farms, and he also backed the controversial idea of 'tenant right' – the right of each outgoing occupier to sell their 'good will' to the incoming tenant, which was customary on some Irish estates.[4]

Soon after Bermingham's open letter to Sir Robert Peel in 1843, a parliamentary commission was established to examine landlord–tenant relations and the possibility of reforming the system of land tenure in Ireland. The Devon commission, as the resulting inquiry became known, gathered information from around the country on this question in 1844. However, dominated as it was by landlords, its report envisioned minimal alteration to existing tenurial arrangements, and, in the words of Peter Gray, 'offered little to cottiers and labourers beyond greater landlord paternalism'.[5] It was not until the Land acts of the late 19th century that Irish tenants would be granted legal rights of the kind suggested by Bermingham in the mid-1840s.

During the 1840s, as well as contributing to and participating in the RAIS and BAIS – organizations that aimed to promote 'agronomy' among Irish landlords and tenants – Bermingham also became involved in the Society for the Improvement of Ireland (Irrespective of Sect or Party). In his words, its object was 'to seek grants and loans of money from the Government, in pursuance of a report of a committee of the House of Commons in February 1835, on Public Works in Ireland, for the furtherance of Irish industry'.[6] Among other projects, the Society for the Improvement of Ireland lobbied for the drainage of the river Suck and its tributaries in east Galway.[7] It was also mentioned in the house of lords in August 1846 when it backed a petition that opposed the introduction of a Spirit Licences and Duties bill.[8] Referring to the failure of this organization in 1847, Bermingham wrote of his role 'as vice-president of a Society for the Improvement of Ireland (short lived, certainly, and ill supported), which put forward many useful publications, and which, under providence, had it been better supported, would have averted a vast deal of the subsequent misery which Ireland had endured'.[9]

In 1847, Bermingham wrote a pamphlet that detailed perhaps his most ambitious scheme, which he advised the government and other interested parties to take heed of in order to alleviate the effects of the Famine that was then ravaging the country. In *The Thames, the Shannon, and the St Lawrence, or the good of Great Britain, Ireland and British North America identified and promoted*, Bermingham elaborated on his idea that if small tenants and cottiers were to be dispossessed of their holdings – a measure recommended by the leading political economists of the day, and one that seemed unavoidable if the potato could not be relied upon to feed the mass of Irish peasants who depended upon it for their sustenance – then employment needed to be provided in order to avoid the starvation and recrimination of those displaced.[10]

With this in mind, Bermingham took it upon himself to identify fourteen economic sectors where employment could be found for 250,000 families, primarily in the areas of infrastructural and agricultural improvement. The main thrust of this plan – unsurprisingly considering his push for railroads at the time of its conception – consisted of the employment of many of Ireland's at-risk labourers and displaced cottiers on the building of an Irish rail network. The other sectors where humanitarian-motivated investment would be profitable in the long run, according to Bermingham, included: the construction of harbours, fishing piers, quays and docks; the deepening of river beds and public drainage; private drainage schemes; building better houses and out offices on demesnes; the construction of boats for deep sea fishing; employment in mines and quarries; the erection of lime kilns; the reclamation of wastelands; building cottages for labourers; the establishment of agricultural schools on model farms and fishing and nautical schools; the drainage and sewage of cities, towns and villages; assessments for making bridges and repairing roads; and the construction of infrastructure in British North America in preparation for mass colonization. By paying the labourers who would complete these projects a fair wage, Bermingham believed that they could save the requisite money to afford passage to Canada or Australia, and to purchase land in those countries, which were themselves then in need of an influx of immigrants. In this way, he maintained that the British empire at large would benefit from investment in Ireland.[11]

Bermingham estimated that this scheme would cost the gigantic sum of £63,500,000 over the following ten years. Moreover, he suggested a novel way to raise this figure; in effect, he argued that Ireland should be incorporated. Bermingham advised the government to create shares called 'the Irish improvement stock', which he maintained would be purchased by Irish landlords, joint stock companies and other interested capitalists, since he believed that the shares would generate ample return in the long run when Ireland recovered from the Famine.[12] Of course, such an idea may now seem fanciful; however, it was a mark of Bermingham's ambition and ego that he was prepared to suggest such a massive and expensive project – one that wove together the various threads of his improving ethos: agricultural reform, the reclamation of wastelands and investment in drainage schemes, infrastructural improvement through the provision of a modern rail network for Ireland, all combined with an exhortation of Irish landlords to assume their responsibilities. Directly addressing Irish landed proprietors when advertising the scheme, he wrote: 'the time has at length arrived, when you can no longer shrink from the performance of those duties which rightly belong to your position in society. Your lot is now cast with proprietors who have long admitted, and acted on the principle, that property has duties as well as rights to attend to'.[13] Here Bermingham echoed Thomas Drummond, the reforming Whig under-secretary stationed at Dublin castle from 1835 to 1841, who controversially reminded

Irish landlords on one occasion that 'property has its duties as well as its rights'.[14] According to Bermingham, Clonbrock and a minority of other progressive and paternalistic Irish landlords already acted on this principle; it was now time for the entire Irish landed class to follow the example of their more 'enlightened' brethren and, with the backing of the government and the co-operation of Ireland's lower classes, to self-modernize *en masse*.

Bermingham's ambitious Famine relief plan was not acted upon, which is unsurprising considering the fact that, in the *laissez-faire* political and economic climate of the 1840s, Westminster balked at even extending the more modest sums suggested by Lord Benthnick and Thomas Redington for the provision of loans to fund Irish railway companies (discussed in chapter two). Nevertheless, the scheme is a telling indication of Bermingham's mindset. He believed that the improvement of Ireland would not only be of insular benefit to the Irish, but also to the United Kingdom and the entire British empire. Investment in pursuit of this end was not only desirable on patriotic and humanitarian grounds, therefore, but was also in the self-interest of Irish landlords and the British nation, since it would lead to long-term peace and stability in Ireland, as well as profits that the Irish farmer could use to purchase manufactured goods produced in the industrial districts of England and Scotland.[15] Thus, for Bermingham, paternalism and profit were not incompatible agendas if a conservative form of modernization was pursued, such as that which he worked for as agent for the Clonbrock estates between 1826 and 1843. In this respect, he was akin to the many British agricultural improvers of his day who held that investment in socially desirable projects could also be economically remunerative.[16]

In November 1849, Bermingham wrote a letter to *The Times* (London) to advertise Irish lands to willing English farmers on behalf of an unnamed Galway landlord. Evictions, mortality, emigration and voluntary relinquishment of holdings in order to qualify for government relief had left vacant farms on many Irish estates. During and after the Famine many landlords moved toward consolidating these small holdings with a view towards 'anglicizing' Irish agriculture, and some proprietors sought British tenants to farm them.[17] In this context, on behalf of an unnamed landlord from Dunmore, Co. Galway, Bermingham wrote to advertise the fact that 'a proprietor of 1,200 acres within two miles of that town, who is now beside me, authorizes me to treat with any Lincolnshire farmer of ability for at least 250 acres of it now in grass, and without population, for a long lease and at fair rent'.[18] This exchange points us towards the new profession that Bermingham entered into in the early 1850s, when he became a buyer in, and a broker for, the Encumbered Estates Court.

The Great Famine (1845–52) was viewed by many contemporaries as incontrovertible evidence that the pre-Famine structure of Irish agriculture had been unviable. Even before the potato blight, most political economists had argued for the need to consolidate Ireland's small tillage holdings, especially in the west and south-west of the country. As discussed in the first chapter,

Bermingham had endeavoured to consolidate farms on the Clonbrock estates between the late 1820s and the early 1840s, but did so in a slow and incremental manner in order to avoid resistance. During the latter years of the Famine this process was accelerated throughout Ireland when some landlords used the crisis as an excuse to clear large swathes of their estates of unwanted small farmers and cottiers, thereby exacerbating the misery, death, and emigration associated with the Great Famine.[19]

In 1849, amid widespread condemnation of Irish landlords for their perceived failures among British politicians and middle classes, the government passed the Encumbered Estates act. This was a measure that facilitated the sale of indebted Irish landed estates to interested buyers. While demand for this land was generally low among the British capitalists whom it was originally envisioned would purchase Ireland's indebted estates and 'anglicize' agriculture thereon – with most of the land bought by existing solvent Irish landlords and members of the Catholic middle class – some English and Scottish investors did avail of the opportunity to buy Irish estates with a view towards turning them into profitable commercial enterprises.[20] Bermingham played a role in this transfer of property. Harnessing his considerable knowledge of Ireland's landed estate system, he became an estate agent for this court.

Irish newspapers of the early 1850s were often replete with advertisements for estates that were sold under the provisions of the Encumbered Estates act. In these notices, Thomas Bermingham was frequently named as a contact for interested parties seeking to obtain detailed information about specific properties. Interestingly, in October 1853, he was named as a broker in the sale of lands formerly belonging to George King at Castlesampson and Iskerbane in county Roscommon – the very places where he had implemented his home colonization scheme two decades earlier.[21] It is unclear whether Clonbrock had sold these townlands to George King, who was then forced to sell them in the Encumbered Estates Court, but if so, it is ironic that Bermingham would have had a role in selling the same lands he had declared improved and solvent while trumpeting his home colonization idea two decades earlier.[22] In 1854 and 1855, he was also involved in the sale of several other estates in counties Kildare, Antrim, Longford, Tipperary, Roscommon and Galway. In these advertisements Bermingham, described as an 'estate agent', could be contacted at addresses in Dublin and London, in order to furnish maps, rentals and other particulars to prospective buyers.[23]

Not only did Bermingham facilitate the sale of indebted Irish estates in this manner, he also bought land through these courts in the early 1850s. In April 1851, he was named as the purchaser of an estate in Gortaleam, near Dunmore, Co. Galway, for the sum of £1,400. In July of the same year he bought an estate in Mountpark, Co. Meath for £10,100.[24] Bermingham was probably a proxy for other buyers in these transactions, since he himself moved to Dublin in these years and took up residence in Sandymount, where he became a justice of the peace.[25] His appointment to this post indicates an elevated social stature; as W.E. Vaughan has noted, justices of the peace were usually drawn from the gentry class in 19th-century Ireland.[26]

As the Encumbered Estates Court was reaching the end of its lifespan in the latter half of 1855, Bermingham saw an opportunity to combine his knowledge of land available for purchase in the courts with his ability to act as a broker on behalf of interested buyers. Noting that there were 40,000 acres of good land still available for sale in Galway, he advertised the idea that a joint stock company, comprised of at least 25 individuals, should come together as a conglomerate, which he would represent, in order to buy and develop this land with a combined sum of roughly £500,000. Bermingham calculated that this venture would yield a return of five per cent after five years for investors. According to the *Tuam Herald*, Bermingham

> who recommends to individual capitalists, for private investment, or for the purpose of forming companies under the new liability act, for the purchase of these estates, is in a position to ascertain the sums required for that purpose by private contract ... with a full intention to secure a fair remuneration for his services.[27]

It appears that nothing came of this idea. Nevertheless, it is a telling example of Bermingham's undiminished ambition that he suggested such a massive undertaking, and his self-belief that he could manage what would have been the gargantuan task of ensuring a return for investors by rationalizing the disparate estates in question and modernizing agriculture thereon, while simultaneously treating the existing residents with respect and humanity.

Perhaps it was better for Bermingham that this idea was not taken up by investors, at least for his reputation. In their attempts to make a profit from their properties, many of the people who purchased Irish land in the Encumbered Estates Court encountered considerable resistance and recrimination during the 1850s. Alan Pollock, for example – a Scottish buyer – earned himself widespread negative publicity for his clearance of estates in east Galway and Roscommon.[28] Bermingham evidently believed that he possessed the expertise to avoid such problems, having promised in the advertisement for his investment opportunity that he would ensure a smooth transition and 'the acquiescence of a peaceable tenantry, in the carrying out of any judicious reforms in the size of farms &c'.[29] In practice, however, notwithstanding his knowledge of the region, it is highly unlikely that Bermingham could have reorganized agricultural holdings on vast tracts of land without encountering the resistance of at least some of those estates' pre-existing 'surplus' inhabitants. On the Clonbrock estates, in the two decades preceding the Famine, Bermingham had acted on behalf of a landlord who had demonstrated patience with incremental progress and was prepared to invest large sums in 'paternalistic' improvements. However, Clonbrock had a vested interest in engaging in even uneconomical spending, since he valued the 'loyalty' of his tenants and his public reputation highly. If Bermingham had acted on behalf of relatively anonymous investors to whom he had promised a return within five years, in the altered context of post-Famine Ireland, where markets prices were influencing a growing preference for livestock farming at the expense of small tillage holdings, he would likely have had to be much more radical in clearing the land and consolidating holdings. Had that happened, Bermingham might well have been targeted for derision which would have sullied the generally positive reputation he had earned during his tenure as agent for the Clonbrock estates and his campaigns for Irish infrastructural improvement.

Conclusion

Throughout his career, Thomas Bermingham was a consistent improver and modernizer, both with regard to the landed estates that he managed and Irish society more generally. Importantly, his vision of improvement was largely conservative in nature. During the 1830s and 1840s, Bermingham dismissed calls for the 'anglicization' of Irish agriculture as impracticable, and looked instead to continental nations such as Belgium, where small farms were proven adequate to support a comfortable peasant class if cultivated intensively. He firmly believed in the benefit that would be wrought by agricultural and infrastructural modernization, but he also maintained that this should not disregard the needs of the poor or the small farmer class, and should not dissolve the bonds of reciprocity that he believed existed between supposedly good landlords and their supposedly loyal tenants. Where those bonds did not exist, as on the estates that belonged to the members of the landed class who thought only of 'pounds, shillings and pence',[1] Bermingham was eager to have the idea of rights and duties enshrined in legislation.[2]

As an agent, Bermingham endeavoured to cast himself as stern but fair, with a view toward effecting the long-term, incremental improvement of his employers' estates and the consequent prosperity of the landlord, the tenants, and the labourers. As a public campaigner, he was persistent in his advocacy of what he saw as the most viable way forward for Ireland's predominantly agricultural economy and society. He demonstrated a willingness to alter his opinion as circumstances changed – evinced by his about-turns on the issues of government funding for Irish rail and the corn laws – even though this earned him a reputation for caprice.

Significantly, there was considerable cross-fertilization between Bermingham's private and public roles. In his position as an agent he became thoroughly acquainted with the wants and needs of Irish landlords, tenants, and labourers, and he was able to advocate the wider adoption of his home colonization, wasteland reclamation and drainage schemes by reference to their supposed utility on the Clonbrock estates. Bermingham's position as agent to a prominent landlord also provided him with the requisite social stature to participate in committees and societies and to publish pamphlets. However, while there was a large degree of positive interaction between his public and private roles, there could also be conflict, as evident during the controversy in which Bermingham became embroiled in 1841 when he publicly called for an alteration in the corn laws. Just as Lord Clonbrock had a reputation to uphold, inherited from his father, so too did Bermingham have the reputations of his own father and uncle to live up to. He called on the names of his forebears to quell the audience at the tumultuous corn law meeting in Loughrea in 1841, reportedly imploring: 'I am, said he, a nephew of H[enry] Grattan, will you hear me now?' In response, someone in the audience replied 'you are a disgrace to him'.[3] In truth, measured against the standards of his day, Bermingham was not a disgrace to either his father or his uncle, exerting himself as he did, even through persistent illness, in the cause of 'improvement'. However, in attempting to combine the roles of both his father and uncle (agent and campaigner), and especially in holding contrary party-political views to Clonbrock, Bermingham encountered some difficulties, since the social convention of his day dictated that his first 'duty' was to represent his employer. Irish land agents, despite becoming a more professional class during the 19th century, were still widely considered to be projections of a landlord's power. Thus, it was only when Bermingham left Clonbrock's employment that he became more explicitly political, moving from exhorting landlords to assume their responsibilities to the argument that they should be compelled to do so through legislation.

In June 1855, Bermingham was absent from the celebration at Clonbrock House that marked the 21st birthday of his former employer's eldest son, Luke Gerald Dillon, future 4th Lord Clonbrock.[4] To acknowledge this occasion, the following month he wrote an open letter to one of Clonbrock's tenants that was published in the *Tuam Herald*. In his letter, Bermingham remarked that he had retired from his position as Clonbrock's agent due to illness, but was happy that he had been replaced by Charles Filgate, whom he characterized as an able and active man. Bermingham also fondly remembered what he considered the halcyon days of the 1830s and early 1840s on the Clonbrock estates, and thoroughly complimented his former employer, noting that 'to instruct the tenantry was his Lordship's delight; witness the several Scotch agriculturalists introduced on the estate for their edification, and long will I, and I am sure you will, remember the Clonbrock ploughmen gaining prize after prize with the "Bridge of Allen" ploughs'.[5]

Thus, the 3rd Baron Clonbrock earned a positive public reputation for his 'improving' ethos, but it was his agents who were actually responsible for implementing that ethos by endeavouring to negotiate a balance between modernization and paternalism in the day-to-day administration of his estates. Although the Irish aristocracy's vision of paternalistic improvement can be rightly criticized for its motives and effects, from the perspective of the landed class Bermingham was a successful agent. Believing that Ireland's agricultural system needed to be reorganized, he oversaw a host of reforms on Clonbrock's behalf that were intended to rationalize estate management, modernize farming, and ensure profitability while simultaneously endeavouring to limit or mitigate the impact of the resulting 'improvements' upon the tenantry. Consequently, the well-known Irish reformer and agent John Pitt Kennedy wrote in 1835 that the examples of Clonbrock and Bermingham indicated: 'Irish landlords and agents can be found who are instruments of good instead of evil to their dependents'.[6] While the binary characterization of landlords and agents as either 'good' or 'evil' is over-simplistic, and although many of the tenants and labourers that Bermingham dealt with in the course of his career might disagree, it is clear that he and Clonbrock did at least try to pursue a version of improvement that was in the interest of both landlord and tenant. Furthermore, their involvement with agricultural societies and infrastructural development suggests that there were Irish landlords and agents who also endeavoured to be instruments of 'good' instead of 'evil' to their country, albeit with crucial biases and failures. How representative Clonbrock and Bermingham were of their respective classes is another question entirely.

Notes

ABBREVIATIONS

BAIS	Ballinasloe Agricultural Improvement Society
Devon commission, part ii	*Evidence taken before her majesty's commissioners of inquiry in respect to the occupation of land in Ireland*, part ii, HC 1845 (616), xx.i.
GIRC	General Irish Railway Committee
Hansard 3	*Hansard's parliamentary debates*, third series, 1830–91 (vols i–ccclvi, London, 1831–91)
HC	House of commons parliamentary papers
JGAHS	*Journal of the Galway Archaeological and Historical Society*
MGWR	Midland Great Western Railroad of Ireland
NLI	National Library of Ireland
Poor inquiry, appendix d	*Poor inquiry (Ireland), appendix d. Baronial examinations relative to the earnings of labourers, cottier tenants, employment of women and children, expenditure, with supplement containing answers to questions*, HC 1836, xxx
Poor inquiry, appendix f	*Poor inquiry (Ireland), appendix f. Baronial examinations relative to conacre, quarter of score ground, small tenantry, consolidation of farms, emigration, landlord and tenant, agriculture, taxation, roads, with supplement containing answers to questions*, HC 1836, xxxiii
RAIS	Royal Agricultural Improvement Society of Ireland

INTRODUCTION

1   Cormac Ó Gráda, *Ireland before and after the Famine: explorations in economic history, 1800–1930* (Manchester, 1988), pp 1–35; Niall Ó Ciosáin, *Ireland in official print culture, 1800–1850: a new reading of the poor inquiry* (Oxford, 2014); R.D. Collison Black, *Economic thought and the Irish question, 1817–1870* (Cambridge, 1960).
2   See R.D. Collison Black, 'The Irish dissenters and nineteenth-century political economy', *Hermathena*, 85 (1983), 120–37; Jennifer Ridden, 'Irish reform between the 1798 rebellion and the Great Famine' in Arthur Burns and Joanna Innes (eds), *Rethinking the age of reform, 1780–1850* (Cambridge, 2003), pp 271–94.
3   *Galway Weekly Advertiser*, 29 May 1841. The term was used in a derisive context on this occasion.
4   Kevin McKenna, 'Power, resistance, and ritual: paternalism on the Clonbrock

estates, 1826–1908' (PhD, NUI Maynooth, 2011); Kevin McKenna, 'Charity, paternalism and power on the Clonbrock estates' in Laurence Geary and Oonagh Walsh (eds), *Philanthropy in nineteenth-century Ireland* (Dublin, 2013), pp 97–114; Patrick Melvin, *Estates and landed society in Galway* (Dublin, 2012), pp 92–6, 246–50.
5   For studies of land agency in Ireland, see Ciarán Reilly, *The Irish land agent, 1830–60: the case of King's County* (Dublin, 2014); Gerard Lyne, *The Lansdowne estate in Kerry under the stewardship of William Steuart Trench, 1849–72* (Dublin, 2001); Mary Delaney, *William Steuart Trench and his management of the Digby estate, King's County, 1857–71* (Dublin, 2012); William Crawford, *The management of a major Ulster estate in the late eighteenth century: the eight earl of Abercorn and his Irish agents* (Dublin, 2001); Desmond Norton, *Landlords, tenants, Famine: the business of an Irish land agency in the 1840s*

(Dublin, 2006); W.E. Vaughan, *Landlords and tenants in mid-Victorian Ireland* (Oxford, 1994), pp 108–13. For a recent volume that situates Irish land agents in British and imperial contexts, see Lowri Ann Rees, Ciarán Reilly and Annie Tindley (eds), *The land agent, 1700–1920* (Edinburgh, 2018).

6 *Dublin Evening Mail*, 31 May 1841.

7 Bermingham was named as Grattan's nephew in *Galway Weekly Advertiser*, 29 May 1841. Corroboration of this fact is contained in Thomas Bermingham, *Statistical evidence in favour of state railways in Ireland* (Dublin, 1841), appendix, p. xciv, where Bermingham thanked his 'kinsman', Henry Grattan MP, son of the famous Irish 'patriot' politician of the same name.

8 See Cormac Ó Gráda, *Ireland: a new economic history, 1780–1939* (Oxford, 1994), pp 69–130; Michael Beames, *Peasants and power: the Whiteboy movements and their control in pre-Famine Ireland* (Sussex, 1983); David Ryan, 'Ribbonism and agrarian violence in county Galway, 1819–1820', *JGAHS*, 52 (2000), 120–34; James S. Donnelly Jr, *Captain Rock: the Irish agrarian rebellion of 1821–1824* (Cork, 2009).

9 *Third report of the commission of inquiry into the condition of the poorer classes in Ireland (poor inquiry)*, HC 1836, xxxi; *Report from her majesty's commissioners of inquiry into the state of the law and practice in respect to the occupation of land in Ireland (Devon commission)*, HC 1845 (605), xix.

10 Thomas Malthus to David Ricardo, 17 Aug. 1817, in Piero Saffra (ed.), *Works and correspondence of David Ricardo, vii: letters, 1816–18* (Cambridge, 1952), p. 175.

11 Gearóid Ó Tuathaigh, *Ireland before the Famine, 1798–1848* (Dublin, 1972), pp 117–26; K. Theodore Hoppen, *Ireland since 1800: conflict and conformity* (2nd ed., New York, 1999), pp 44–5; Denis O'Hearn, *The Atlantic economy: Britain, the US and Ireland* (Manchester, 2001), pp 80–106.

12 Robert Torrens, *Self-supporting colonization; Ireland saved, without cost to the imperial treasury* (London, 1847); Kerby Miller, *Emigrants and exiles: Ireland and the Irish exodus to North America* (Oxford, 1985), pp 193–279; Gerard Moran, *Sending out Ireland's poor: assisted emigration to North America in the nineteenth century* (Dublin, 2004).

13 Samuel Madden, *Reflections and resolutions proper for the gentlemen of Ireland* (Dublin, 1738); William Conner, *The true political economy of Ireland; or, Rack-rent, the one great cause of all her evils, with its remedy* (Dublin, 1835); William Blacker, *An essay on the best mode of improving the condition of the labouring classes of Ireland* (London, 1846); Robert Kane, *The industrial resources of Ireland* (Dublin, 1844); William Sharman Crawford, *A defence of the small farmers of Ireland* (Dublin, 1839).

14 On British political economists' discussions of Ireland in the first half of the 19th century, see Black, *Economic thought and the Irish question*, pp 15–44; Thomas Boylan and Tadhg Foley, *Political economy and colonial Ireland: the propagation and ideological function of economic discourse in the nineteenth century* (London, 1992).

15 See, for example, Thomas Skilling, *The science and practice of agriculture* (Dublin, 1846), pp 35–9; Joseph Lambert, *Agricultural suggestions to the proprietors and peasantry of Ireland* (Dublin, 1845). On Irish land agents' admiration for Belgian agriculture, see Reilly, *The Irish land agent*, p. 85.

16 Enda Delaney, *The curse of reason: the Great Irish Famine, 1845–52* (Dublin, 2012), pp 35–8, 166–84; Ciarán Ó Murchadha, *The Great Famine: Ireland's agony, 1845–52* (London, 2011).

17 William Blacker, *An essay on the improvements to be made in the cultivation of small farms, by the introduction of green crops and housefeeding the stock thereon* (Dublin, 1833).

18 See Jonathan Bell and Mervyn Watson, *Irish farming: implements and techniques, 1750–1900* (Edinburgh, 1986).

1. THOMAS BERMINGHAM, PROFESSIONAL LAND AGENT

1 See J.E. Pomfret, *The struggle for land in Ireland, 1800–1923* (Princeton, 1930); James S. Donnelly Jr, 'Landlords and tenants' in W.E. Vaughan (ed.), *A new history of Ireland, v: Ireland under the union, 1801–70* (Oxford, 1989), pp 332–49;

Vaughan, *Landlords and tenants in mid-Victorian Ireland*.

2 James S. Donnelly Jr, *The land and the people of nineteenth-century Cork: the rural economy and the land question* (London, 1975), pp 51–72; Hoppen, *Ireland since 1800*, pp 38–9; W.A. Maguire, *The Downshire estates in Ireland, 1801–1845: the management of Irish landed estates in the early nineteenth century* (Oxford, 1972); Gerard Moran, *Sir Robert Gore Booth and his landed estate in county Sligo, 1814–1876: Famine, emigration, politics* (Dublin, 2006).

3 Cathal Smith, 'Second slavery, second landlordism, and modernity: a comparison of antebellum Mississippi and nineteenth-century Ireland', *Journal of the Civil War Era*, 5:2 (June 2015), 204–30.

4 Maria Edgeworth, *The absentee* (Dublin, 1812); William Carleton, *Valentine McClutchy, the Irish agent; or, The chronicles of Castle Cumber* (Dublin, 1845).

5 K. Theodore Hoppen, *Elections, politics and society in Ireland, 1832–1885* (Oxford, 1984), pp 137–44; Reilly, *The Irish land agent*, pp 36–71; Maguire, *The Downshire estates in Ireland*, pp 183–216; Norton, *Landlords, tenants, famine*, p. 1. On the Irish middleman system, see David Dickson, 'Middlemen' in Thomas Bartlett and D.W. Hayton (eds), *Penal era and golden age: essays in Irish history, 1690–1800* (Belfast, 1979), pp 162–85.

6 See Donnelly, *The land and the people of nineteenth-century Cork*, pp 173–87; Reilly, *The Irish land agent*, pp 120–45; Lyne, *The Lansdowne estate in Kerry under the stewardship of William Stuart Trench*; Padraig Vesey, *The murder of Major Mahon, Strokestown, county Roscommon, 1847* (Dublin, 2008).

7 *Devon commission*, part ii, p. 512.

8 Melvin, *Estates and landed society*, pp 20–2; *Freeman's Journal*, 1 June 1790.

9 U.H.H. de Burgh, *The landowners of Ireland: an alphabetical list of the owners of estates of 500 acres or £500 valuation and upwards in Ireland* (Dublin, 1878), p. 87.

10 Correspondence, 1815 (NLI, Grattan papers, MS 27,802); *Report of the select committee on the state of Ireland, with the minutes of evidence, appendix, and index*, HC 1831–32 (677), xvi, p. 456.

11 See Conor McNamara, '"The monster misery of Ireland": landlord paternalism and the 1822 famine in the west' in Laurence Geary and Oonagh Walsh (eds), *Philanthropy in nineteenth-century Ireland* (Dublin, 2015), pp 89–90.

12 *Freeman's Journal*, 19 Apr. 1828.

13 Notice written by Lord Clonbrock, 8 Nov. 1830, in estate, farm and household account books of the Clonbrock estates (NLI, Clonbrock papers, MS 19,507).

14 Estate, farm and household account books of the Clonbrock estates, 1827–33 (NLI, Clonbrock papers, MS 19,507).

15 Notices written by Thomas Bermingham, 2 May 1827, 15 June 1827, in estate, farm and household account books of the Clonbrock estates (NLI, Clonbrock papers, MS 19,507).

16 See Clonbrock cash books, 1833–46 (NLI, Clonbrock papers, MS 19,508).

17 Melvin, *Estates and landed society*, p. 93.

18 *Report of the select committee on the state of Ireland*, pp 455–6.

19 Melvin, *Estates and landed society*, pp 110, 208, 254.

20 *Report of the select committee on the state of Ireland*, p. 468.

21 *Poor inquiry*, appendix f, p. 143.

22 Ibid.

23 McKenna, 'Charity, paternalism and power', 102–3; *Report of the select committee on the state of Ireland*, p. 466; *Poor inquiry*, appendix d, pp 1–2.

24 Note written by Thomas Bermingham, Oct. 1831, in estate, farm and household account books of the Clonbrock estates, 1827–33 (NLI, Clonbrock papers, MS 19,507).

25 *Report of the select committee on the state of Ireland*, p. 463. On the Terry Alts, see James S. Donnelly Jr, 'The Terry Alt movement of 1829–31', *History Ireland*, 2 (1994), 30–5.

26 For discussions of paternalism on the Clonbrock estates, including Bermingham's role in the practical execution of this ideology of reciprocity, see McKenna, 'Power, resistance, and ritual', pp 17–51; McKenna, 'Charity, paternalism and power', pp 97–114; Melvin, *Estates and landed society*, pp 211–12; Cathal Smith, 'Lords of land and labour: a comparison of antebellum

Mississippi's John A. Quitman and nineteenth-century Ireland's Lord Clonbrock' (PhD, NUI Galway, 2015), pp 109–95.

27 Barak Longmate, *Stockdale's peerage of England, Scotland and Ireland: containing an account of all the peers of the United Kingdom, ii: peerage of Scotland and Ireland* (London, 1810), p. 329; Bernard Burke, *Burke's genealogical and heraldic history of the peerage, baronetage and knightage of Great Britain* (London, 1861), p. 1122.

28 According to an 1827 letter, 'the death of Lady Wallscourt gives the third of the Bermingham estate to my Lord Clonbrock, the rental of which is about £3,920 ... the one third being his Lordship's proportion will be £1,225 10s.' Letter to Lord Clonbrock, 5 June 1827 (NLI, Clonbrock papers, MS 35,758 (3)).

29 General statements of agent's accounts, 1837 (NLI, Clonbrock papers, MS 35,724 (11)). According to this document the Limerick estate was sold for £30,300, the Westmeath property for £17,150, and the Tipperary holding for £1,700. The cost of purchasing the Ballydonelan estate was estimated at £66,545, while the net costs of the Castlegar, Doone, and Dalystown estates were recorded as £24,465, £16,181 5s., and £29,300 respectively.

30 Smith, 'Second slavery, second landlordism, and modernity', p. 214.

31 For information on Luke Dillon's drainage efforts, see Hely Dutton, *A statistical and agricultural survey of the county of Galway, with observations on the means of improvement; drawn up for the consideration and by the direction of the Royal Dublin Society* (Dublin, 1824), p. 18.

32 For sums spent on the drainage and reclamation of bog and wasteland at Doone, see rentals and accounts of the Clonbrock estates, 1834–40 (NLI, Clonbrock papers, MS 19,596, MS 19,598, MS 19,600, MS 19,602, MS 19,604, MS 19,606, MS 19,608).

33 *Poor inquiry*, appendix f, p. 359.

34 W. Reed to Thomas Bermingham, 28 Jan. 1835, in Thomas Bermingham, *The social state of Great Britain and Ireland considered, with regard to the labouring population* (London, 1835), p. 137.

35 See Katherine Hull, 'To drain and to cultivate: agriculture and "improvement" at Ballykilcline' in Charles Orser (ed.), *Unearthing hidden Ireland: historical archaeology at Ballykilcline, county Roscommon* (Bray, 2006).

36 *Freeman's Journal*, 27 Sept. 1837.

37 *Tuam Herald*, 2 Oct. 1841.

38 Caesar Otway, *A tour in Connaught* (Dublin, 1839), p. 163.

39 *Devon commission*, part ii, p. 507.

40 Thomas Bermingham, *Report on the state of the river Shannon, both as to the navigation and the drainage of the adjoining lands: together with a report on the lakes of Galway and Mayo* (London, 1831), p. 5.

41 Thomas Bermingham, *Short narrative of the home colonies of Castle-Sampson and Iskerbane, established for the rt. hon. Lord Clonbrock, upon his estates in the county of Roscommon, in Ireland* (London, 1833). On the rundale system, see Desmond McCourt, 'The decline of rundale, 1750–1850' in Peter Roebuck (ed.), *Plantation to partition: essays in Ulster history in honour of J.L. McCracken* (Belfast, 1981), pp 119–39.

42 Bermingham, *Report on the state of the river Shannon*, pp 3–4.

43 *Poor inquiry*, appendix f, 80.

44 Bermingham, *Short narrative of the home colonies of Castle-Sampson and Iskerbane*, pp 3–4.

45 Bermingham, *Social state of Great Britain and Ireland*, pp vi–viii; McKenna, 'Power, resistance, and ritual', p. 18.

46 *Poor inquiry*, appendix f, p. 80.

47 Bermingham, *Short narrative of the home colonies of Castle-Sampson and Iskerbane*, p. 4. Robert Wilmot Horton was a British politician who advocated Irish emigration to Canada during the 1820s.

48 Ibid.; McKenna, 'Power, resistance, and ritual', pp 18–21.

49 Martin Doyle, *The works of Martin Doyle, i: an address to the landlords of Ireland, on subjects connected with the melioration of the lower classes* (Dublin, 1835), p. 81. Doyle also published a full account of Bermingham's home colonization scheme, which he recommended other Irish landlords to emulate. Ibid., pp 128–35.

50 Bermingham, *Social state of Great Britain and Ireland*, p. 145.

51 For examples of compensation to tenants for undertaking improvements on their holdings over the course of Bermingham's agency of the Clonbrock estates, see Rentals and accounts of the Clonbrock estates, 1827–43 (NLI, Clonbrock papers, MS 19,585–19,614).

52 Blacker, *An essay on the improvements to be made in the cultivation of small farms*; Martin Doyle, *The works of Martin Doyle: hints originally intended for the small farmers of the county of Wexford; but suited to the circumstances of most parts of Ireland* (Dublin, 1831); Jonathan Bell and Mervyn Watson, *A history of Irish farming, 1750–1950* (Dublin, 2008).

53 See Smith, 'Second slavery, second landlordism, and modernity', pp 216–20.

54 Blacker, *An essay on the improvements to be made in the cultivation of small farms*.

55 *Tuam Herald*, 1 Oct. 1842.

56 *Poor inquiry*, appendix f, p. 359.

57 Rentals and accounts of the Clonbrock estates (NLI, Clonbrock papers, MS 19,606, MS 19,608, MS 19,610, MS 19,612); McKenna, 'Power, resistance, and ritual', pp 66–7.

58 *Tuam Herald*, 17 Oct. 1840; Rentals and accounts of the Clonbrock estates (NLI, Clonbrock papers, MS 19,600, MS 19,604, MS 19,606, MS, 19,608); McKenna, 'Power, resistance, and ritual', p. 64.

59 Doyle, *Address to the landlords of Ireland*, p. 25.

60 *Poor inquiry*, appendix f, p. 206.

61 See Reilly, *The Irish land agent*, pp 84–95.

62 Rentals and accounts of the Clonbrock estates, 1827–43 (NLI, Clonbrock papers, MS 19,585–19,614).

63 Thomas Bermingham to Lord Clonbrock, 16 Apr. 1841, in summary of the cash accounts of the Clonbrock demesne, 1841 (NLI, Clonbrock papers, MS 35,732 (1)).

64 See Terence Dooley, *The decline of the big house in Ireland: a study of Irish landed families, 1860–90* (Dublin, 2001), pp 151–7; Vaughan, *Landlords and tenants in mid-Victorian Ireland*, pp 33, 104.

65 Rentals and accounts of the Clonbrock estates, 1828 (NLI, Clonbrock papers, Ms 19,586). For more sums paid to

Bermingham for the duration of his agency, see rentals and accounts of the Clonbrock estates, 1827–43 (NLI, Clonbrock papers, MS 19,585–19,614).

66 See letters from Thomas Bermingham to Robert Dillon, 3rd Baron Clonbrock, with associated items of correspondence relating to the purchase of land and the administration of the Clonbrock estate, 1829–43 (NLI, Clonbrock papers, MS 35,727 (9)).

67 Thomas Bermingham to Lord Clonbrock, 13 Jan. 1842 (NLI, Clonbrock papers, MS 35,727 (9)).

68 For more on Bermingham's opinion of the Irish poor law, see Thomas Bermingham, *Remarks on the proposed poor law bill for Ireland, addressed to George Poulett Scrope, esq., member for Stroud* (London, 1838).

69 McKenna, 'Charity, paternalism and power', pp 104–7; McKenna, 'Power, resistance, and ritual', pp 37–47; *Tuam Herald*, 31 Mar. 1838 (quotation). On the Irish poor law, see Peter Gray, *The making of the Irish poor law, 1815–43* (Manchester, 2009).

70 *Second appendix to reports relative to the valuations for poor rates, and to the elective franchise in Ireland*, HC 1842 (326), xxiii, p. 177.

71 Mr Ponsonby to Thomas Bermingham, 15 May 1833 (NLI, Clonbrock papers, MS 35,731 (1)).

72 Thomas Bermingham to Dr Kinchela, 23 Feb. 1835, in Bermingham, *Social state of Great Britain and Ireland*, p. 215.

73 *Freeman's Journal*, 17 Apr. 1839.

74 Bermingham, *Statistical evidence in favour of state railways*, p. 5; D. Farrell to Thomas Bermingham, 22 Feb. 1842 (NLI, Clonbrock papers, MS 35,727 (9)).

75 *Tuam Herald*, 14 July 1855.

76 John Hull, *The philanthropic repertory of the plans and suggestions for improving the condition of the labouring poor* (London, 1841), p. 68.

2. 'THE PROPHET AND THE PROJECTOR':
THOMAS BERMINGHAM, CAMPAIGNER AND
PAMPHLETEER

1 See Virginia Crossman, *Politics, law and order in nineteenth-century Ireland* (Dublin,

1996), pp 49–76; Ó Tuathaigh, *Ireland before the Famine*, pp 88–114; D. George Boyce, *Nineteenth-century Ireland: the search for stability* (2nd ed., Dublin, 2005), pp 63–104.

2 Oliver MacDonagh, 'Economy and society, 1830–45' in Vaughan (ed.), *A new history of Ireland*, v, pp 218–41; Donnelly, *The land and the people of nineteenth-century Cork*, pp 9–72.

3 Bermingham, *Short narrative of the home colonies of Castle-Sampson and Iskerbane*; Bermingham, *Report on the state of the river Shannon*, p. 4 (quote).

4 Doyle, *Address to the landlords of Ireland*, pp 80–1.

5 McKenna, 'Power, resistance, and ritual', p. 23; Rentals and accounts of the Clonbrock estates, 1835, 1838 (NLI, Clonbrock papers, 19,596, MS 19,598).

6 Donnelly, *The land and the people of nineteenth-century Cork*, pp 58–9.

7 Bermingham, *Correspondence between Sir Robert Peel and Thomas Bermingham*, 8.

8 Bermingham, *Statistical evidence in favour of state railways*, p. 18. W.E. Vaughan has estimated that, in post-Famine Ireland, average landlord expenditure on improvements was as low as 4 per cent of rent receipts, and calculated that the figure for the Clonbrock estate stood at 10 per cent in the 1850s; however, this was after Bermingham had left Clonbrock's employment, and the figure was doubtlessly higher in the 1830s. See Vaughan, *Landlords and tenants in mid-Victorian Ireland*, pp 123, 277.

9 Thomas Bermingham, *Letter addressed to the right honourable Lord John Russell: containing facts illustrative of the good effects from the just and considerate discharge of the duties of a resident landlord in Ireland, with practical suggestions for legislative enactments necessary to induce, if not compel, the fulfillment of similar duties by all landlords* (London, 1846), p. 6; Jonathan Binns, *The miseries and beauties of Ireland* (2 vols, London, 1837), ii, p. 10.

10 *Poor inquiry*, appendix f, p. 133.

11 Ibid.; Rentals and accounts of the Clonbrock estates, 1836 (NLI, Clonbrock papers, MS 19,600); McKenna, 'Power, resistance, and ritual', pp 22, 45–6, 107–8; Moran, *Sending out Ireland's poor*, p. 137.

12 Bermingham, *Letter addressed to the right honourable Lord John Russell*, p. 7.

13 *Western Star*, 20 Mar. 1847.

14 Bermingham, *Social state of Great Britain and Ireland*, p. 127; Bermingham, *Letter addressed to the right honourable Lord John Russell*, pp 6–7; McKenna, 'Power, resistance, and ritual', p. 22.

15 *Poor inquiry*, appendix f, p. 80; Binns, *Miseries and beauties of Ireland*, ii, pp 17–18.

16 Cormac Ó Gráda, 'Poverty, population, and agriculture, 1801–45' in Vaughan (ed.), *A new history of Ireland*, v, pp 128–9.

17 For a detailed account of the foundation meeting of the Royal Agricultural Improvement Society of Ireland on 18 Feb. 1841, see *Dublin Evening Mail*, 19 Feb. 1841.

18 *First report of the royal agricultural improvement society of Ireland* (Dublin, 1841), p. viii; *Second report of the royal agricultural improvement society of Ireland* (Dublin, 1841), pp 3, 67.

19 *Tuam Herald*, 17 Oct. 1840; Melvin, *Estates and landed society*, pp 94–5; Cathal Smith, 'Apostles of agricultural reform: the Ballinasloe agricultural improvement society in an era of high farming and famine, 1840–1850', *JGAHS*, 64 (2012), 128–45.

20 Bermingham, *Social state of Great Britain and Ireland*, p. 21.

21 McDonough, 'Economy and society', p. 221; Ó Gráda, *Ireland: a new economic history*, p. 123; Bell and Watson, *History of Irish farming*, pp 16–17; Reilly, *The Irish land agent*, pp 92–3; Smith, 'Second slavery, second landlordism, and modernity', p. 219.

22 Smith, 'Apostles of agricultural reform', pp 141–2.

23 Hull, *Philanthropic repertory*, p. 68; John Pitt Kennedy, *Instruct; employ; don't hang them: or, Ireland, tranquilized without soldiers, and enriched without English capital. Containing observations on a few of the chief errors of Irish government and Irish landed proprietors, with the means of their correction practically illustrated* (London, 1835), p. vi.

24 *First report of the committee on the western rail-road and navigation company* (Dublin, 1831), pp 2–10.

25 Thomas Bermingham, *Additional statements on the subject of the river Shannon to the reports published in 1831* (London, 1834), pp 3–4; Bermingham, *Report on the state of the river Shannon.*

26 Bermingham, *Additional statements on the subject of the river Shannon*, pp 11, 14.

27 *Tuam Herald*, 11 Dec. 1841. See also Bermingham, *Statistical evidence in favour of state railways*, p. 5.

28 Tom Ferris, *Irish railways: a new history* (Dublin, 2008), pp 8–9.

29 Rail was first used in the drainage of Doone bog in 1835; that year Clonbrock paid £42 14s. 8d. for the freight of rail from England for this purpose. See right honourable Lord Clonbrock's separate account with Thomas Bermingham, 1835–36 (NLI, Clonbrock papers, MS 19,598).

30 Thomas Bermingham, *First report and proceedings of the general railway committee, appointed at a public meeting held at the commercial buildings, on Friday, the 22nd day of November, 1838* (Dublin, 1838).

31 *Second report of the commissioners appointed to consider and recommend a general system of railways for Ireland (Drummond commission)*, HC 1837–38 (145), xxxv; Ferris, *Irish railways*, pp 9–12; Thomas Bermingham, *A letter to the rt. hon. Lord Viscount Morpeth from Thomas Bermingham, esq., of Caramana, Kilconnell, county Galway, chairman of the general Irish rail-road committee: upon the advantages certain to accrue to Ireland by the introduction of railway communication to the river Shannon, and to other parts of the kingdom* (London, 1839).

32 Thomas Bermingham, *A report of the proceedings at two public meetings, held at the Thatched House Tavern on the 13th and 20th of April 1839, for the purpose of taking into consideration the necessity of forming railways throughout Ireland* (London, 1839), pp 4, 7.

33 Bermingham, *Report of the proceedings at two public meetings*, pp 6–7. For more on Bermingham's belief that employment was the key to pacifying Ireland, see Bermingham, *Social state of Great Britain and Ireland*, p. 11.

34 Bermingham, *Report of the proceedings at two public meetings*, pp 3–8.

35 *Railway Times*, 25 May 1839.

36 *Railway Times*, 25 May 1839.

37 Bermingham, *A report of the proceedings at two public meetings*, p. 7.

38 Thomas Bermingham, *A statistical account of foreign and English railways; extracted from synopsis of German railways, and from the Statistical Journal of London, as referred to by able articles in the Railway Times and Mining Journal of Saturday, May 18, 1839* (London, 1839), p. 24.

39 Ibid., pp 11–15; Thomas Bermingham, *Irish railways: a full and interesting report of the public proceedings on this important question: with extracts from the statistical journals of the day* (London, 1839).

40 Bermingham, *Statistical evidence in favour of state railways*, pp 7–8.

41 *Tuam Herald*, 11 Dec. 1841.

42 Bermingham, *Irish railways*, p. 47.

43 See Ernest Shepherd, *The midland great western railroad of Ireland: an illustrated history* (Leicester, 1994).

44 *Galway Vindicator*, 9 Oct. 1847.

45 Thomas Bermingham, *The Thames, the Shannon, and the St. Lawrence, or the good of Great Britain, Ireland and British North America identified and promoted by the employment of 250,000 families of the destitute peasantry of Ireland improperly called redundant population* (London, 1847), p. ii; *Tuam Herald*, 16 Dec. 1848, 10 Mar. 1849.

46 See Oliver Byrne to Thomas Bermingham, Feb. 1845, in *The civil engineer and architect's journal, scientific and railway gazette, volume vii, 1845* (London, 1845), p. 62.

47 *Western Star*, 22 Jan. 1848.

48 *Western Star*, 9 Sept. 1848.

49 *Western Star*, 16 Sept. 1848.

50 Bermingham, *The Thames, the Shannon, and the St Lawrence*, p. vii.

51 William Hunt and Reginald Poole (eds), *The history of England, during the reign of Victoria, 1837–1901* (New York, 1907), p. 77; Peter Gray, *Famine, land and politics: British government and Irish society, 1843–1850* (Dublin, 1999), pp 271–2, 317.

52 Ó Tuathaigh, *Ireland before the Famine*, p. 122.

53 *Tuam Herald*, 10 Mar. 1849, 2 June 1849.

54 *Galway Mercury*, 2 Sept. 1849, 2 Aug. 1851.

55 *Tuam Herald*, 14 July 1855.

56 John Cunningham, *A town tormented by the sea: Galway, 1790–1914* (Dublin, 2004), p. 166; James Mitchell, 'Father

Peter Daly (c.1788–1868)', *JGAHS*, 39 (1983/84), 54–5. For an account of a public meeting that honoured Anthony O Flaherty for his exertions in bringing rail to Galway, see *Tuam Herald*, 9 Aug. 1851.

57 *Freeman's Journal*, 5 Aug. 1851; *Tuam Herald*, 10 Jan. 1852 (quote); *Nenagh Guardian*, 17 Jan. 1852.

58 Thomas Bermingham, *A letter from Thomas Bermingham, esq., to the people of Ireland: particularly to the inhabitants of the provinces of Leinster & Connaught, on the subject of the Irish great western railway from Dublin to Galway: with three explanatory maps* (London, 1845), p. 2.

59 *Galway Mercury*, 6 Dec. 1851. Also see *Tuam Herald*, 16 Aug. 1851, 3 Jan. 1852.

60 Camillo Benso Cavour, *Thoughts on Ireland: its present and its future* (2nd ed., London, 1868), p. 82. For more on Cavour's analysis of conditions in Ireland, see Enrico Dal Lago, 'Count Cavour's 1844 *Thoughts on Ireland*: liberal politics and agrarian reform through Anglo-Italian eyes' in Niall Whelehan (ed.), *Transnational perspectives on modern Irish history* (London, 2015), pp 88–105.

61 Bermingham, *Letter addressed to the right honourable Lord John Russell*, p. 19.

62 *Tuam Herald*, 22 Mar. 1851.

63 Shepherd, *The midland great western railroad of Ireland*, p. 17. For more on the MGWR's involvement with the push for Galway to become a center of transatlantic trade, see George Willoughby Hemans, *Mr Heman's report on the port of Galway as a packet station, in communication with America, to the directors of the midland great western railway* (Dublin, 1850).

64 Cunningham, *A town tormented by the sea*, p. 172.

65 Timothy Collins, 'The Galway Line in context: a contribution to Galway maritime history, part 1', *JGAHS*, 46 (1994), 1–42; Timothy Collins, 'The Galway Line in context: a contribution to Galway maritime history, (concluded)', *JGAHS*, 47 (1995), 36–86; Cunningham, *A town tormented by the sea*, pp 172–7.

66 See Bermingham, *Report on the state of the river Shannon*, p. 5; Bermingham,

Social state of Great Britain and Ireland, p. 161; Bermingham, *Statistical evidence in favour of state railways*, p. 16, appendix r; Bermingham, *Report of the proceedings at two public meetings*, p. 11; Bermingham, *Letter addressed to the right honourable Lord John Russell*, pp 30–2.

67 Nassau Senior, *Journals, conversations and essays relating to Ireland* (2 vols, London, 1868), i, p. 131.

68 *Tuam Herald*, 11 Dec. 1841.

69 In 1863, Clonbrock was listed as a shareholder in the MGWR with shares valued at over £2,000. See *Report of the midland great western railway of Ireland company's thirty sixth half yearly meeting* (Dublin, 1863) (in NLI, Clonbrock papers, MS 35,816 (4)).

70 Lord Clonbrock to John Blakeney, 21 Feb. 1861 (NLI, Clonbrock papers, MS 35,758 (4)).

71 *Freeman's Journal*, 5 Aug. 1851.

72 See Peter Solar, 'Shipping and economic development in nineteenth-century Ireland', *Economic History Review*, 59 (2006), 717–42.

3. 'A FALLEN POLITICIAN':
BERMINGHAM AND THE CORN LAW
CONTROVERSY OF 1841

1 Bermingham, *Statistical evidence in favour of state railways*, pp 8–9.

2 Bernard Semmel, *The rise of free trade imperialism: classical political economy, the empire of free trade and imperialism, 1750–1850* (Cambridge, 1970); Paul Pickering and Alex Tyrell, *The people's bread: a history of the anti-corn law league* (London, 2000); Norman McCord, *The anti-corn law league, 1838–1846* (London, 1958).

3 See *Connaught Journal*, 19 Mar 1840.

4 *Tuam Herald*, 22 Feb. 1839; *Tuam Herald*, 30 Mar. 1839.

5 *Connaught Journal*, 19 Mar. 1840.

6 Thomas Bermingham, *A letter on the corn laws, addressed to the land owners and occupiers of land in Ireland: with extracts from Mr. Jacob's report on foreign agriculture and foreign corn* (Dublin, 1841).

7 William Blacker, *The claims of the landed interests to legislative protection considered; with reference to the manner in which the manufacturing, commercial, and agricultural*

classes contribute to national wealth and
prosperity (London, 1836), pp 131–53.
8 Bermingham, *Letter on the corn laws*, p. 5.
9 *Dublin Evening Mail*, 31 May 1841.
10 *Galway Weekly Advertiser*, 29 May 1841.
11 *Tuam Herald*, 29 May 1841.
12 *Tuam Herald*, 5 June 1841.
13 Bermingham, *Letter on the corn laws*, pp
   4–5; *Dublin Evening Mail*, 31 May 1841.
14 *Tuam Herald*, 29 May 1841.
15 *Dublin Evening Mail*, 28 May 1841, 2 June
   1841.
16 *Galway Weekly Advertiser*, 29 May 1841.
17 *Galway Weekly Advertiser*, 5 June 1841.
18 *Dublin Evening Mail*, 28 May 1841.
19 *Tuam Herald*, 5 June 1841.
20 *Dublin Evening Mail*, 31 May 1841.
21 *Dublin Evening Mail*, 2 June 1841.
22 *Dublin Evening Mail*, 31 May 1841.
23 *Tuam Herald*, 5 June 1841.
24 *Dublin Evening Mail*, 2 June 1842.
25 *Tuam Herald*, 12 June 1841.
26 *Dublin Evening Mail*, 28 May 1841.
27 *Tuam Herald*, 14 July 1855.
28 *Nenagh Guardian*, 17 Jan. 1852.
29 *Dublin Evening Mail*, 2 June 1841.

4. BERMINGHAM AFTER CLONBROCK

1 Bermingham, *Correspondence between
   Sir Robert Peel and Thomas Bermingham*,
   p. 5. For more on Bermingham's view
   of the Union, and his belief that it was
   only valid if based on mutual interest,
   see *Western Star*, 17 Apr. 1847. On
   the Repeal movement, see Lawrence
   McCaffrey, *Daniel O'Connell and the
   Repeal year* (Lexington, 1966).
2 Bermingham, *Letter addressed to the right
   honourable Lord John Russell*, pp 5, 14.
3 Bermingham, *Correspondence between Sir
   Robert Peel and Thomas Bermingham*, pp 8,
   16.
4 Bermingham, *Letter addressed to the right
   honourable Lord John Russell*, p. 8. On
   'tenant right', see Vaughan, *Landlords and
   tenants in mid-Victorian Ireland*, pp 67–102.
5 Gray, *Famine, land and politics*, p. 71.
6 *Nenagh Guardian*, 18 Mar. 1846,
7 *Nenagh Guardian*, 21 Mar. 1846.
8 *Hansard 3*, lxxxviii, col. 751, 17 Aug. 1846.
9 *Western Star*, 17 Apr. 1847.
10 Bermingham, *The Thames, the Shannon,
   and the St Lawrence*.

11 Ibid., pp 15–22.
12 Ibid., pp 22–5.
13 Ibid., p. viii.
14 Thomas Drummond to the earl of
   Donoughmore, 22 May 1838, in
   John F. McLennan (ed.), *Memoir of
   Thomas Drummond, under-secretary
   to the lord lieutenant of Ireland, 1835 to
   1840* (Edinburgh, 1867), p. 322. On
   Drummond, see Gearóid Ó Tuathaigh,
   *Thomas Drummond and the government of
   Ireland, 1835–41* (Dublin, 1977).
15 Bermingham, *The Thames, the Shannon,
   and the St Lawrence*, pp 26–7.
16 See Kenneth Hudson, *Patriotism with
   profit: British agricultural societies in the
   eighteenth and nineteenth centuries* (London,
   1972).
17 Donnelly, *The land and the people of
   nineteenth-century Cork*, pp 116–17.
18 *The Times*, 7 Nov. 1849.
19 See James S. Donnelly Jr, *The great Irish
   potato Famine* (Glouchestershire, 2001),
   pp 153–61; James S. Donnelly Jr, 'Mass
   eviction and the Great Famine: the
   clearances revisited' in Cathal Póirtéir
   (ed.), *The Great Irish Famine* (Dublin,
   1995), pp 155–73; Ó Murchadha, *The
   Great Famine*, pp 113–34.
20 Gray, *Famine, land and politics*, pp 200–23;
   Donnelly, *Great Irish potato Famine*, pp
   163–8. For an account of the operation
   of the Encumbered Estates Court in
   Galway, see Pádraig Lane, 'The impact
   of the Encumbered Estates Court upon
   the landlords of Galway and Mayo',
   JGAHS, 38 (1981/2), 45–58.
21 *Freeman's Journal*, 12 Oct. 1853.
22 Bermingham mentioned the possibility
   of selling Castlesampson in a letter to
   Clonbrock in 1840. George King was
   a large tenant of Clonbrock's who is
   frequently referred to in the Clonbrock
   estate accounts; therefore, it is possible
   that King bought Castlesampson and
   Iskerbane from Clonbrock. See Thomas
   Bermingham to Lord Clonbrock, 23
   Nov. 1840 (NLI, Clonbrock papers,
   Ms 35,727 (9)); The right honourable
   Lord Clonbrock's private accounts
   with Thomas Bermingham, 1839, 1841,
   1842, 1843 (NLI, Clonbrock papers,
   MS 19,606, MS 19,610, MS 19,612, MS
   19,614).

23 *Freeman's Journal*, 1 Apr. 1854, 2, 5, 22
May 1854, 14, 17 Aug. 1854, 1, 9, 16 Nov.
1854, 22 Jan. 1855, 18 June 1855, 1, 20
Oct. 1855.

24 *Freeman's Journal*, 16 Apr. 1851, 12 July
1851.

25 'Grantham Villa, Blakeney Parade,
Sandymount, Dublin' was the address
annexed to Bermingham's open letter to
John Carr in 1855, as it also was when
he advertised himself as a broker for
the purchase of 40,000 acres of land in
Galway. See *Tuam Herald*, 14 July 1855,
29 Sept. 1855. The same year he also sent
a letter to a meeting about a bridge in the
Sandymount locality, signed 'Thomas
Bermingham, JP.' See *Freeman's Journal*,
23 Oct. 1855.

26 Vaughan, *Landlords and tenants in mid-
Victorian Ireland*, p. 6.

27 *Tuam Herald*, 29 Sept. 1855.

28 Pauline Scott, 'Rural radicals or
mercenary men? Resistance to evictions
on the Glinsk/Creggs estate of Allan
Pollock' in Brian Casey (ed.), *Defying

the law of the land: agrarian radicals in Irish
history* (Dublin, 2013), pp 65–79; Pádraig
Lane, 'Purchasers of land in counties
Galway and Mayo in the Encumbered
Estates Court, 1849–1858', *JGAHS*, 43
(1991), 106–7.

29 *Tuam Herald*, 29 Sept. 1855.

CONCLUSION

1 Bermingham, *Correspondence between Sir
Robert Peel and Thomas Bermingham*, p. 8.

2 Bermingham, *Letter addressed to the right
honourable Lord John Russell*, p. 5.

3 *Galway Weekly Advertiser*, 29 May 1841.

4 See *Tuam Herald*, 16 June 1855; Kevin
McKenna, 'Elites, ritual, and the
legitimation of power on an Irish landed
estate, 1855–90' in Ciaran O'Neill (ed.),
Irish elites in the nineteenth century (Dublin,
2013), pp 68–82.

5 *Tuam Herald*, 14 July 1855.

6 Kennedy, *Instruct; employ; don't hang them*,
p. 12.